SECRETS
OF THE
LABYRINTH

SECRETS
OF THE
LABYRINTH

Greg Mosse

This edition first published in Great Britain in 2007 by
Orion Books,
an imprint of The Orion Publishing Group Ltd,
Orion House, 5 Upper Saint Martin's Lane,
London, WC2H 9EA

1 3 5 7 9 10 8 6 4 2

A CIP catalogue record for this book is
available from the British Library.

ISBN 978 0 75288 865 1

Printed in Italy by Printer Trento

The Orion Publishing Group's policy is to use papers
that are natural, renewable and recyclable products and made
from wood grown in sustainable forests. The logging and
manufacturing processes are expected to conform to the
environmental regulations of the country of origin.

www.orionbooks.co.uk

Als Catars

Figeac

R. Lot

Marmande

Casseneuil

R. Aveyron

R. Garonne

Agen

Bruniquel

Cordes

R. Tarn

Albi

Rabastens

Lombers

Lavaur

Auch

St Paul-Cap
de-Joux

Toulouse

Muret

St-Félix
Laurgais

Hautpont

Les Cassès

Avignonet

Saissac

Auterive

Castelnaudary

Cabaret

Boulbonne

Trèbes

Bram

Prouille

Carcassonn

R. Gers

Fanjeaux

R. Garonne

Pamiers

Mirepoix

Limoux

R. Ariège

Laroque
d'Olmes

Alet

Arques

Foix

Puivert

Coustaussa

Lombrives

Montségur

Lordat

Roquefeuil

Peyrepertuse

Ax

Montaillou

P Y R E N E E S

ANDORRA

Canigou

S P A I N

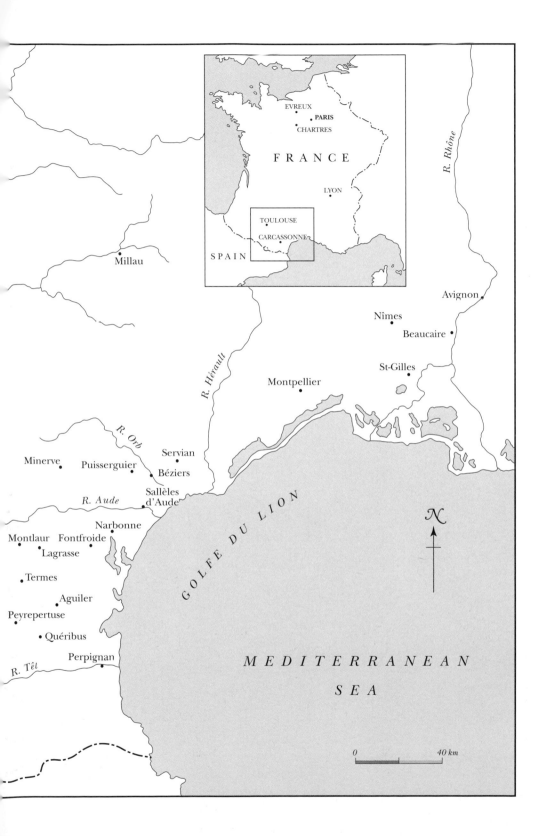

EVREUX
PARIS
CHARTRES

F R A N C E

LYON

TOULOUSE
CARCASSONNE

S P A I N

R. Rhône

Millau

Avignon

Nîmes
Beaucaire

St-Gilles

R. Hérault

Montpellier

R. Orb

Minerve   Servian
     Puisserguier
          Béziers

R. Aude

Sallèles
d'Aude

Narbonne

Montlaur   Fontfroide
     Lagrasse

Termes

Aguiler

Peyrepertuse

Quéribus

Perpignan

R. Têt

GOLFE DU LION

N

M E D I T E R R A N E A N

S E A

0   40 km

⌘ CONTENTS ⌘

The Wheel Turns

Trapped

Reborn

⌘ PROLOGUE ⌘

We bought a tiny house in Carcassonne in 1989, almost by chance, knowing nothing about the place. It turned out that our modest home from home had been built with stones salvaged from the walls of the decaying medieval Cité.

Everywhere we went in Languedoc – that country within a country in southwest France – I came face to face with the past. History seemed alive in the vast sweep of the Pyrenees, the isolated hill towns and *bastides*, the living rivers and the majestic Canal du Midi. The Languedoc, past and present, slipped into my imagination.

In those early years, in a haphazard way, little more than a tourist still, I read to learn more about the place we increasingly called home – guidebooks, history books, old photographs, museum catalogues. I visited the so-called Cathar castles and discovered that the ruined fortresses had been several times rebuilt, that there had been an attempt to cleanse the land of its authentic indigenous history. So my reading became a little more detailed, more complex. I discovered controversies of interpretation – even of fact.

In 1992, with my husband and daughter, I went to Montségur. We took the mountain way. We drove south out of Carcassonne through Limoux – beautiful in summer with its central square and rocky river winding through the town – and turned right towards Puivert. The pale spring sun gave way to grey rain, then sleet. The road twisted and turned until we felt carsick, dizzy and disorientated.

By the time we got to the village of Montségur, snow was sticking to the windscreen and visibility was down to a few metres. We found somewhere to park and unpacked ourselves from the fuggy, steamed-up car. The peak itself was invisible, hidden in the snow clouds. Everything appeared closed, but we did find one empty restaurant. Two dogs lying in front of an open fire. Long, polished refectory tables, beautiful framed photographs on all the walls, in between the bricks and the beams. When the owner appeared, it felt almost rude to ask for lunch. But he was delightful and turned out to be George Serrus, the author of one of the many guidebooks about Montségur I'd got stacked up on my shelves.

In April 1996, we went back, this time with two children rather than one. And as I climbed to the citadel alone, out of the corner of my eye I imagined a woman who would become Alaïs, the central medieval character of *Labyrinth*, pictured her standing on the icy walls in a long red cloak.

As the imagined sequence of events in my novel developed, in my mind's eye I saw the books of secrets she and others had vowed to conceal. I studied the lost language of the pharaohs – my maternal grandmother was half-Egyptian – and found that, as Alaïs stood on the wall of Montségur, the skill of reading the 'divine writing' had been lost for nearly 800 years. And I thought about who it would be who lit the flames down there on the *prat dels cremats* – the 'field of the burned'. I met the power brokers of medieval Christianity in Rome and Cîteaux, determined to impose their orthodoxy. I saw the French king, hungry for land in the prosperous southwest. I saw the brutal genocide they employed to achieve their goals.

But still I asked myself why. And to answer the question, I looked further back into history, to the foundation of Carcassonne in the European Stone Age. I followed the medieval Crusaders to the Holy Land and looked back to the time of David and Solomon, kings of the Jews, and the building of the Temple. I saw Jerusalem fall to the siege of a Muslim caliph just a few short years after the death of the Prophet Mohammed. I imagined Charlemagne camped beneath the walls of Carcassonne, home to a Saracen princess. But despite the fact that my research ranged over nearly 5,000 years of history and three continents – Europe, Asia and Africa – it always led me back to the Cité on the Hill.

So that is where we shall start...

Kate Mosse
Carcassonne, January 2007

CHAPTER 1

The Cité on the Hill

etween the mountains of central France and the Pyrenees, there is a wide and fertile corridor of land. It stretches from the vast and sandy estuary at Bordeaux, where the Garonne and the Dordogne meet the Atlantic, to the lagoons and salt-marshes of the Mediterranean Golfe du Lion at modern Narbonne. In between, there are two great cities. Toulouse is one, nicknamed *la ville rose* for the pink stone used to build its oldest streets and squares. The other, 90 kilometres to the southeast, was founded on a hilltop near a medium-sized river around 3500 BCE, almost unimaginably distant in time. Today, it is called Carcassonne.

The people who lived on that hilltop by the river Aude were Neolithic – Stone Age – digging and hunting with broken shards of rock and flint – and would do for another 2,000 years. Then, with the passing of the generations, trade routes were established. Technology for making bronze tools arrived from the East. Narbonne became a crossroads, where the long coastal highway linking the eastern and western Mediterranean joined the route north through the Carcassonne gap to the Atlantic.

Six hundred years before the dawn of the Christian era, Carcassonne was at last becoming – recognisably – the Cité on the Hill. It was fortified by a tribe of Gauls called the Volcae, originally from the Rhine valley but whose capital was now at the site of modern Toulouse. The Volcae and their brother tribes grew to dominate an area that corresponds very closely to the medieval territory of Languedoc. Around the same time in the Holy Land, Nebuchadnezzar's Babylonians sacked Jerusalem, destroyed the Temple and enslaved the Israelites; in Persia, the prophet Zarathustra founded his dualist philosophy – Zoroastrianism – which saw Creation as a battleground between good and evil forces.

The first great European empire was beginning to organise and expand. With each new area of conquered land, a Roman *provincia* – province – was created. In 121 BCE, the *provincia* of Gallia Narbonensis was formed from the Volcae lands, giving Rome control of the land route between Italy and the Iberian Peninsula and access to the north through the Carcassonne gap. With their customary engineering brilliance, more than a hundred years before Christ, they built the Via Domitia, the Roman road from Italy across southern Gaul to Spain. Around the same time, they made the Via Aquitania, the road northwest through Carcassonne to Bordeaux. It has since been replaced by a motorway, the Autoroute des Deux Mers, that funnels traffic between the Mediterranean and the Atlantic.

Though they surrendered, the Volcae remained independent. Their leaders negotiated with their conquerors to obtain the *ius Latii*, a special status granted to particular Roman colonies – not full citizenship but with more rights than the *peregrines* – the provincials. The Romans added their own fortifications to the Cité on the Hill. Provinces like Gallia Narbonensis were a buffer, protecting the Roman homelands in the peninsula of modern Italy from attack by Gaulish or Germanic tribes.

Around 58 BCE, Julius Caesar was governor of two of the buffer *provinciae*. Soon, with the unexpected death of the governor of Gallia Narbonensis, he acquired a third. He set out with four veteran legions under

In Narbonne today, a fragment of the Via Domitia can still be seen in front of the Hôtel de Ville.

his direct command. Some historians think that he planned to march northeast to plunder the Balkans. Instead he marched north, perhaps attracted by the contrasting Gaulish attributes of wealth and tribal division. A sequence of successful military campaigns eventually took the northern frontier of the Roman Empire to the Scottish border.

Carcassonne, in the heart of Caesar's *provincia* of Gallia Narbonensis, was upgraded to become a strategic *colonia* – an outpost – and renamed Julia Carcaso, later Carcasum. Extensive remnants of the Gallo-Roman fortifications can still be seen today, especially at the northern end of the Cité. Meanwhile, the independence of the Celtic Volcae declined as they became more and more Roman themselves.

Julius Caesar amassed conquests and plunder. In 49 BCE, accused of treason, he marched towards Rome and broke Roman law by crossing the river Rubicon with the 13th Legion. On taking this fateful decision, Caesar is supposed to have said: '*Iacta alea est.*' ('The die is cast.')

And so it was, for it marked the end of the Roman Republic and the beginning of empire, the start of a parabola of rise and fall that would see

Roman language, law, technology and customs – including, at different times, persecution, toleration and encouragement of Christianity – embedded in the colonised societies of vast domains. At its greatest, in about the year 117 of the Christian era, it stretched from Scotland to the Persian Gulf and from Tangier on the threshold of the Atlantic to the Sea of Azov in Central Asia.

From this point, the Roman Empire began slowly to wane. In 268 CE, the Goths, a Germanic people originally from Sweden, advanced victorious through the Roman Balkans and threatened the homeland of *Italia* itself. They were defeated on the Italian–Slovenian border but not repelled from all the lands they had taken. As the years passed, Rome also had to consider the strengthening threat from the forces of the Franks from the lands we now call Belgium and northern France.

The old *provincia* of Gallia Narbonensis was divided in two, east and west. The western portion containing Carcassonne and Béziers – most of the lands that we call Languedoc – was named Septimania. But the reorganisation changed nothing – Roman authority was failing. By 462 CE decline had become fall. Septimania was ceded to the control of the western Visigoths and the fortifications at Carcassonne were extended. It may have been the Visigoth king Theodoric II who first built a church on the site of the basilica of Sant-Nasari in the Cité.

The Visigoths built a capital in Toulouse and an empire that stretched from southern Portugal, east to Italy and north to the valley of the Loire. They were Arian Christians. (They did not believe in a Holy Trinity composed of three equal parts – God the Father, God the Son and the Holy Spirit. They saw Jesus as a separate being, created by God, after God.) They too came under pressure from the Franks, who pushed them out of Aquitaine. The Visigoths moved their capital to Ravenna in Italy, then to Barcelona and then Toledo in the safety of distant southern Spain. But there they faced the belligerence of the Byzantine emperor Justinian I, the inheritor of the throne of the Eastern Roman Empire. Soon they would have to face the still mightier threat of Muslim military expansion.

With Visigoth society under military pressure, disputes between church and army became common. When the Visigoth king Reccared converted to Catholicism, he took it upon himself to declare that all Jews must abjure their faith and be baptised, on pain of banishment. Nearly 600 years later, a Catholic pope would choose a different target for another barbaric programme of religious cleansing, launching a genocidal Crusade of

Christian against Christian in the heart of southern Europe. The old Roman and Visigoth outpost of Carcassonne would find itself at the epicentre of that calamity.

CHAPTER 2

'Divine Writing'

Carcassonne, the Cité on the Hill, was founded by Stone Age hunter-gatherers around 3500 BCE. There was no writing – tradition and knowledge were passed down by word of mouth. At the same time, in the valleys of the Tigris and the Euphrates in modern Iraq, history was being recorded in cuneiform script, one of the oldest forms of written expression. In Egypt, there were cities and planned irrigation, not just the annual flood of the Nile fertilising the plains with its nutritious silt.

The climate at that time was different. Scientists believe that the period from 5000 to 3000 BCE may have seen the best, most fertile climatic conditions that the planet has ever enjoyed – a climatic optimum. In that distant past, the temperature was one or two degrees warmer than today and fresh water from rainfall was plentiful – the Nile was three times its present volume.

The first records of hieroglyphic writing, using pictures that stand for words and sounds and ideas, date from at least this long ago. And the Egyptians aren't the only early Bronze Age people to have used pictorial writing. So did the Chinese and the ancient civilisation of Anatolia in eastern Turkey. The Maya of Central America used symbolic writing, much of it written on tree bark, which rotted in the damp of the rainforest or was destroyed by the *conquistadores* from Spain, who considered these symbols to be the work of the Devil. Historians of the Maya have to rely mostly on writing carved into the stone of their buildings.

The ancient Egyptians carved their hieroglyphs into rock and clay too. They dressed their buildings and monuments with stories and bureaucratic records and, thanks to the dry climate, many of these have survived to the present day. They also used papyrus, from which we get our word 'paper'.

Papyrus is a fresh-water reed that still grows in the marshes alongside the Nile. It was the symbol of the kingdom of Lower Egypt. It grows about 3

瞳 旽 暾 暐 曀

Chinese is another language that uses pictographs. The five shown here are: sun about to rise; morning sun or sunrise; sun above the horizon; bright shining sun; and sun hidden by clouds. Notice the shape for sun – 日 – on the left of each character. Early study of the Rosetta Stone led to the bizarre assumption that China had once been a distant colony of Egypt.

metres tall, when it is harvested and the outer leaves pulled away and discarded. The core is sliced as thinly and as widely as possible – the closer to the yellow-white heart of the plant, the better.

The strips are soaked, beaten and rinsed to remove excess sugar, then laid out flat, slightly overlapping one another. A second layer is placed carefully on top, at right angles to the first, and the papyrus is pounded, then left for days under a heavy stone slab. The little sugar that is left in the strips binds them together. When dry, the sheet can be prepared for writing by polishing, often with a piece of shell, bone or ivory.

Sheets of papyrus could be bonded together like this to create a long scroll or, as the years passed, it became more common to cut individual sheets and bind them together in the form of a book that we call a codex. Usually the hieroglyphs were only drawn on one side of the papyrus – the side with the horizontal strips.

Although papyrus was a valuable commodity – its production was made a state monopoly – enormous quantities were produced. Old pieces served for making spills for lighting fires or lamps or were used to pack mummies or even discarded en masse on rubbish heaps covered by the arid sand.

The word 'hieroglyph' comes from a Greek word meaning 'sacred carving' or 'sacred writing'. The original Egyptian phrase – usually written as *'medew-netjer'* – means 'divine words'. Because Egyptian hieroglyphs were incomprehensible for so long, they acquired a sense of deep mystery – as if they must have been designed to conceal secrets rather than to communicate. There were even people who thought that hieroglyphs might conceal eyewitness accounts of the Creation of the world. In fact, they were used to record the details of people's everyday lives, to draw up and publish accounts, to set down important events and records details of harvest or taxes, to praise the mighty and to communicate knowledge across the years.

Understanding hieroglyphs is made difficult by the way that Egyptian writing evolved. It developed into two quite different forms – hieratic, or 'priestly', and demotic, meaning 'used by the people'. Also, there are three types of symbol. There are individual symbolic pictures that stand for people, places, animals or ideas. Then some hieroglyphs represent individual sounds, rather like an alphabet, which can be combined to make words. Lastly, there are symbols – sometimes a single stroke – that modify the meaning of the hieroglyph next to it.

As early as the 4th century CE, few people had any knowledge of how to read hieroglyphs. For most of the previous 1,000 years the lands of the Nile had been ruled by foreigners – Persians, Macedonians and Romans. The final nail in the coffin of ancient Egyptian literature was the compulsory closing of all non-Christian places of worship by the Roman emperor Theodosius I in 391 CE. The last known dated hieroglyphic writing comes from the far south of the kingdom and is thought to date from soon after.

Into this vacuum of knowledge, some wild misjudgements flowed. A 5th-century text, the *Hieroglyphica of Horapollo*, claimed to decipher around 200 hieroglyphs, mostly quite falsely, but the book acquired authority and for perhaps 1,000 years hindered more realistic study. But the *Hieroglyphica of Horapollo* did ensure that the imagery of hieroglyphs wasn't altogether lost in Europe and redesigns of its 200 hieroglyphs figured prominently in Renaissance works of art, and many related books were published around the turn of the 17th century. But no real progress in properly understanding the language of ancient Egypt was made until a belligerent Corsican-French general, in the service of the French Revolutionary government, took it into his head to invade North Africa with an army of soldiers and scientists.

The general was Napoleon Bonaparte, but his role in jeopardising the secrets of the labyrinth lay far in the future.

⌘ CHAPTER 3 ⌘
Jerusalem, the Temple and the Ark

*J*erusalem is an ancient city of the eastern Mediterranean – or of the far west of Asia. It depends on your point of view. It is central to the story of the genocide of the Cathars because before the Albigensian Crusade came the Crusades to the Holy Land.

Jerusalem is set at altitude. Some of its hills reach over 800 metres above sea level. It stands on a watershed, the land where the waters divide, deciding whether to flow westwards down to the open Mediterranean or eastwards into the landlocked Dead Sea. It was founded in the early Bronze Age, a time of great technological advance, around 3000 BCE. That was perhaps 500 years after the unification of Egypt and the settlement of the hilltop that would become Carcassonne.

No one is certain how the city got its name. Biblical commentators look back to Abraham, the father of Israel, who came to the place called Shalem after rescuing his nephew Lot from the sack of Sodom. The Hebrew version is '*Yerushalayim*', sometimes translated as 'heritage of Salem' or 'heritage of peace'. '*Shalem*' means 'whole' or 'in harmony'; '*shalom*' means 'peace'. But, in the medieval period, Jerusalem became a theatre of war, sucking in pilgrims and Crusaders from throughout Europe, mobilising rival Muslim forces and displacing and persecuting the Jews.

For years Jerusalem was home to the Ark of the Covenant, a sacred chest built according to God's instructions, revealed to Moses, to shelter the stone tablets carved with the Ten Commandments. On the lid of the chest were two cherubim through whom Moses could apparently communicate with God. During the Israelites' wanderings, their priests carried the Ark before the people. It opened a pathway through the waters of the Jordan and was borne in procession about the walls of Jericho, eventually bringing them crashing to the ground.

The power of the Ark was such that it was always concealed, wrapped in a veil, in badger skins and a blue cloth. Even the priests – who carried it on long poles pushed through golden hoops – were not allowed to touch it or look upon it.

More than 1,500 years later, the Ark would be mentioned in the Qur'an in the story of Saul, the great unifying king of the Israelites who reigned before David:

*T*heir prophet said to them: 'The sign of his kingship is that the Ark of the Covenant will be restored to you, bringing assurances from your Lord, and relics left by the people of Moses and the people of Aaron. It will be carried by the angels. This should be a convincing sign for you, if you are really believers.'

As a reward for killing the giant Goliath, Saul gave David command of all his armies, then became jealous and planned to have him killed. Saul's son Jonathan – who 'loved David as his own soul' – warned David, who fled into the wilderness. Saul felt deserted by God and relapsed into heathen practices. When his sons were slain in battle with the Philistines, he killed himself.

Civil war followed, with David emerging victorious, acclaimed as a warrior, musician and poet, credited with authorship of many of the psalms. His capture of Jerusalem was confirmed by the entry of the Ark of the Covenant into the city to the sound of harps and cymbals, with David dancing before it.

David planned to build a temple for the Ark and assembled building materials on Mount Moriah, one of the hills of Jerusalem, between Mount Zion to the west and the Mount of Olives to the east. The site David chose and purchased was a threshing floor on a windy rock plateau where the breeze was used to separate the light chaff from the heavier grains of wheat. He set up an altar there and certain Old Testament traditions came to be associated with the place. People began saying it was the exact spot where Adam, the first man, was created from a spoonful of dust. And it was to Mount Moriah that Adam returned on his expulsion from Eden to till the land from which he had been made. In this place, too, Cain slew Abel, and Abraham prepared to sacrifice his son Isaac. (Muslims believe that it was Abraham's elder son, Ishmael, and not Isaac who was offered for sacrifice, and that it took place in Mecca, not Jerusalem.)

A 16th-century fresco depicting David dancing before the ark.

David was succeeded by Solomon, his son, who set out to complete his father's plans using '100,000 talents of gold and 1,000,000 talents of silver' left him by David for the purpose. He acquired huge blocks of stone for the foundations and walls of the Temple from quarries beneath the city. He reached a pact with Hiram I, king of Tyre, who sent him skilled master builders and supplies of timber from the forests of Lebanon. The walls were smoothly jointed limestone – like the ice-white surfaces of the Great Pyramid more than a millennium before. The porch to the Temple was gilt with gold and could be seen throughout the city. Many of the blocks of stone were cut and shaped far from Mount Moriah, then assembled carefully and – above all – quietly on site, so as not to disturb the atmosphere of the sanctuary. The workmen carved huge cisterns into the hill, fed by channels from the 'pools' near Bethlehem. The greatest held 3 million gallons of water.

The Temple was completed in the eleventh year of Solomon's reign, seven and a half years after it had been begun, but stood empty and unused for thirteen years – no one knows why. Finally, the Temple was dedicated and the Ark of the Covenant was processed from its tent to the sanctuary – a Holy of Holies – within the Temple. When, later, Solomon married Pharaoh's daughter, he insisted that she live outside Zion as the city was consecrated by the presence of the Ark. The Holy of Holies, hidden beyond the Temple veil, was entered only once a year by the high priest.

King Solomon was believed to have the power to exorcise evil spirits 'by the aid of some wonderful herb he was acquainted with'. The Bible tells us that he took 700 wives and 300 concubines. One of these was the unnamed Queen of Sheba. Ethiopian legend has it that Menelik, their son, stole the Ark of the Covenant from the Temple in Jerusalem and took it back with him to Ethiopia. If this is so, the Ark of the Covenant would have survived the sack of the city and Temple by Nebuchadnezzar's Babylonians in 597 BCE.

After the Babylonian defeat, the Jews spent several decades in captivity. Then, around 515 BCE, the Persian king Cyrus II overcame Babylon and allowed the Jews to return and rebuild Jerusalem and its Temple. Intriguingly, Cyrus also restored to them their 'sacred vessels'. With the Temple at its heart, prosperous Jerusalem was a prize worth fighting for. Soon war – decisive war – would come. Would the power of the Ark be mobilised once more in its own defence? Time would tell.

CHAPTER 4
The Fall of Rome

*I*n the West, the city of Jerusalem was taking on an almost mystical significance. From his home in Tunis, the Roman Tertullian asserted: 'It is evident from the testimony of even heathen witnesses that in Judea there was a city suspended in the sky early every morning for forty days. As the day advanced, the entire figure of the walls would gradually wane.'

When the Jews returned from exile in Babylon, they rebuilt their holy city, including a greatly expanded Second Temple. As the high priest performed his holy offices in the sanctuaries, his steps and gestures were said to mirror those of the Archangel Michael in Heaven.

Relative peace endured and so did the Second Temple, throughout the rise and expansion of the Roman Empire. Then, in 70 CE, the seventieth year of the Christian era, it was utterly destroyed as a Roman reprisal for the Great Jewish Revolt. Since then, Jews have prayed that God will allow the construction of a Third Temple, possibly alongside the coming of the Messiah.

For 300 years more Jerusalem was under Roman control. In 313 CE, the Emperor Constantine legalised Christianity throughout the empire. Five Catholic bishops had positions of special authority: Rome, Alexandria, Antioch, Constantinople and Jerusalem. These bishops were also known as patriarchs – 'fathers' – and Rome and Constantinople were first among equals. Rome had the authority of its imperial past and the fact that it had been the seat of St Peter, the disciple of Jesus thought of as the first pope. Constantinople was the 'New Rome', the current seat of imperial power.

In the late 4th century CE, Theodosius the Great made Christianity the Roman state religion. Then, when Theodosius died in 395 CE, the vast empire was divided into east and west, each under its own emperor.

Turmoil followed. Unrest and conflict in the mechanisms of state led to division and argument in the church. A council of bishops was convened to discuss and settle matters of doctrine and practice.

The council took place in the autumn of 451 CE at Chalcedon – now part of the city of Istanbul on the Asian side of the Bosphorus. It lasted nearly a month and, at its conclusion, the priests and theologians published the Chalcedonian Creed, an 'infallible' statement of belief. It said, among other things, that Jesus was 'perfect in divinity and perfect in humanity, the same truly God and truly man…like us in all things but sin'.

To this day, the Chalcedonian churches – Roman Catholic, Eastern Orthodox and most Protestants – believe that Christ was fully divine yet fully made a man. The Cathars, on the other hand, would believe that every aspect of the material world was created by Satan and that Christ had never taken flesh.

In any case, this unity did not last. The language of the West was Latin but the language of the East was Greek – and fewer and fewer people were able to understand both. The Eastern Roman Empire, also known as the Byzantine Empire, continued to thrive but, by the end of the 5th century, the Western Roman Empire had been overrun. Tribes of Germanic Huns, Vandals, Ostrogoths and the Visigoths who became lords of Carcassonne took its place. The two churches began to travel different paths, their beliefs and their rites evolving in different ways. As time passed, independence bred distrust. Each side claimed authority and trivial arguments – such as whether to use leavened or unleavened bread in the Eucharist – became major controversies.

Once more, Jerusalem was a prize to be fought over. Constantinople refused to tolerate the presence of Jews within the walls. The pope in Rome claimed he held authority over the four Eastern patriarchs. For Constantinople, the power of Rome was only honorary – a throwback of tradition.

But neither remnant of the great Roman Empire would be able to hold on to the elusive 'city suspended in the sky'. Soon a new religion would arise, announced in the sands of Arabia to an Arab merchant with an unimpeachable reputation for probity, who would visit Jerusalem and its 'farthest mosque' in a vision: the Prophet Mohammed.

☷ CHAPTER 5 ☷
Mohammed

The Prophet Mohammed, founder of Islam, was born in Mecca around 570 CE. Within 150 years a Muslim army of 'Saracens' would join decisive battle in the valley of the Loire and a 'Saracen princess' would reign over Carcassonne.

At about forty years old, Mohammed fell into a trance and had a vision of an ethereal being that he later identified as the Archangel Gabriel. Gabriel told Mohammed that he was the 'messenger of God'. This began a series of revelations which continued until Mohammed's death in 632. (Around 650, the revelations of Mohammed were assembled in written form in the Qur'an. Until that time, his teachings were passed on by word of mouth.)

Mohammed claimed he had been given a mission to 'perfect and complete' the other 'religions of the Book' – Judaism and Christianity. Like most prophets, Mohammed was first ignored then attacked, eventually being forced to flee Mecca for Medina, the world's first true Muslim community. After eight years of war, Mohammed's forces conquered Mecca and its people accepted Islam. In March 632, following the Haj pilgrimage, Mohammed fell ill. He died on 8 June.

Although succession was immediately disputed, the territories of the Muslim Empire began inexorably to expand. In 637 CE, the forces of Caliph Umar – who was with Mohammed when he died – took Jerusalem by siege. The Christian patriarch Sophronius, who traced his succession back to James the Just, brother of Jesus, head of the first Christian church in Jerusalem, gave Umar the keys to the city and invited him to pray at the church of the Holy Sepulchre, but Umar declined, for fear of undermining the church as a Christian temple. He prostrated himself nearby.

Sophronius died soon after Jerusalem fell, but not before negotiating very

Muslims believe that the Shetiyah, *the rock in the centre of the Dome, is the exact location of Mohammed's ascent to God, accompanied by the Angel Gabriel.*

limited religious autonomy for Christians, dependent on payment of a poll tax. They engaged to use clappers in their churches very softly, not to build new places of worship, and to allow old ones to fall into ruin. They promised not to teach the Qur'an to their children or give shelter to spies; not to manifest their religion publicly or convert anyone to it; not to prevent any kin from entering Islam; not to seek to resemble Muslims in dress or hairstyle or speech or honorific names; not to mount on saddles or carry arms; not to engrave Arabic inscriptions on their seals or sell fermented drinks; not to display crosses or holy books in the roads or markets of the Muslims or show lights there; not to bury their dead near Muslims or raise their voices in church services, in the presence of Muslims or when following their dead; not to take slaves allotted to Muslims; not to build houses over-topping the houses of the Muslims; to show respect towards Muslims and rise from their seats if a Muslim wished to sit.

Fifty-five years later, around 690 CE, the mosque of Umar was built on the site where he prayed, the location of the ruins of the Second Temple. The building is now more commonly known as the Dome of the Rock. The mosque was built by Christian Byzantine craftsmen sent from Constantinople. Around twenty years later, another mosque was built nearby, to commemorate the Qur'an story of a miraculous journey undertaken by the Prophet Mohammed from a 'sacred mosque' in Mecca to 'al-Masjid al-Aqsa' – the 'farthest mosque'. The location of the 'farthest mosque' is never spelt out – in fact, the Qur'an never mentions Jerusalem at all – but it has come to be associated with the city.

For over 400 years Jerusalem was a Muslim city. The ruins of the First and Second Temples remained hidden beneath sacred Muslim shrines. Throughout that time, for Christians, Jerusalem remained a place of spiritual pilgrimage, the backdrop to the life and passion – the martyrdom – of Jesus. For the Jews, it remained the city of David, the heart and capital city of their homeland.

Then, on 15 July 1099, the city was conquered by the Catholic Christian soldiers of the First Crusade, including Raymond IV, count of Toulouse, a lord of Languedoc, who wrote: 'If you want to know what was done to the enemies we found in the city, know this; that in the portico of Solomon and in his Temple, our men rode in the blood of the Saracens up to the knees of their horses.'

CHAPTER 6

Saracen Carcassonne

*I*n the seventy years after the death of Mohammed, Muslim evangelism and conquest expanded into Palestine, Syria, Mesopotamia, Persia, Egypt and North Africa. Then their ships bridged the narrow divide of the Strait of Gibraltar and they invaded Visigoth Spain.

The Visigoths were ill-prepared for the challenge. By 718 almost all of Iberia was under Muslim rule. Visigoth power was split into rival kingships – the traditional Arian faction on the one hand and the Catholic converts on the other. Many Visigoths fled north across the Pyrenees into Languedoc and Aquitaine. Some of them were absorbed into the armies of the Franks. The kingdom of the inheritors of Rome had endured for 250 years.

Many histories of the medieval period refer to these Muslim forces – like Raymond IV of Toulouse describing the massacre in the Temple 300 years later – as Saracens. 'Saracen' is a term that was used in the early Roman Empire to describe a tribe of Arab nomads from Sinai. It became, by extension, a way of referring to all Arab peoples. Muslims from North Africa, Spain and Portugal are also often called – like Shakespeare's Othello – 'Moors'.

The army of Saracens advanced across the Pyrenees from Barcelona in 725 and took control of the fortified hill city of Carcassonne. Their forces moved north, seizing much of what we now think of as southern France. Within a generation they came under attack from the Carolingian dynasty of the Franks.

The founder of the Carolingian kings was, in his official title, 'Mayor of the Palace'. His name today is Charles Martel, but he was known to Latin scribes of the time as Carolus Martellus – Charles the Hammer. He was born in what is now Belgium and ruled vast lands from Brittany across northern France, Luxemburg, Belgium and Germany and south into Burgundy.

A 16th century portrait of Charlemagne, by Albrecht Durer.

Charles the Hammer prevented the remorseless Muslim advance from moving any further north. He assembled an army to meet and defeat an Islamic force at Tours in the Loire valley in 732, decisively ending Muslim expansion. When he died, his lands were divided between two of his three sons. Carloman took over the eastern portion of his realm – roughly equivalent to modern Germany. Pépin le Bref took over the western throne, including a large portion of modern France.

Pépin is often referred to in English as Pippin the Short – either of stature or of reign. In fact, his name means Pippin the Younger. He was for a time commander of the Frankish garrison in Toulouse. In 759, he marched south and captured the great port city of Narbonne and took control of nearly all of Aquitaine. But, according to legend, he failed to dislodge the Saracen forces from the fortified Cité on the Hill. The task was passed on to his son and heir, known to contemporary Latin chronicles as Carolus Magnus, or Charles the Great.

We know him as Charlemagne.

⌘ CHAPTER 7 ⌘

Charlemagne

Charlemagne, the grandson of Charles the Hammer, became king of the Franks in 768. He made his capital at Aachen, or Aix-la-Chapelle, on the contemporary border between Belgium and Germany, building an enormous palace whose chapel had the proportions of a cathedral. Einhard, a servant and chronicler of the life of Charles the Great, wrote in *Vita Caroli Magni*:

His height is well known to have been seven times the length of his foot; the upper part of his head was round, his eyes very large and animated, nose a little long, hair fair, and face laughing and merry. Thus his appearance was always stately and dignified, whether he was standing or sitting; although his neck was thick and somewhat short, and his belly rather prominent; but the symmetry of the rest of his body concealed these defects…next to his skin a linen shirt and linen breeches, and above these a tunic fringed with silk; while hose fastened by bands covered his lower limbs, and shoes his feet, and he protected his shoulders and chest in winter by a close-fitting coat of otter or marten skins.

Charlemagne's sword was called *Joyeuse* – 'Joyful' – but he loathed show. The chronicler says: 'He despised foreign costumes, however handsome, and never allowed himself to be robed in them, except twice in Rome.'

Charlemagne was a devout Catholic. He led an army to northern Italy in 772 to defend Pope Hadrian I from Lombard invaders. (Five centuries later, the Cathar church in Lombardy would provide an asylum for the persecuted *Bons Chrétiens* of Languedoc.) Charlemagne was granted the title 'patrician' – an echo of the noble ruling class of Rome. Military victory made him king of the Lombards and *de facto* ruler of Italy.

Next, Charlemagne embarked on a successful thirty-year campaign to subdue and convert to Christianity the people of Saxony in the Rhine valley and beyond. By the end of the campaign of militarised evangelism Einhard noted:

The war that had lasted so many years was at length ended by their acceding to the terms offered by the King; which were renunciation of their national religious customs and the worship of devils, acceptance of the sacraments of the Christian faith and religion, and union with the Franks to form one people.

In the midst of the war in Saxony, Charlemagne was persuaded into an alliance by Saracen emissaries from Spain. He led an army across the Pyrenees and fought a desperate battle at Zaragoza. He decided to retreat, no longer confident of his Moorish allies, but was ambushed by Basque forces in a mountain pass, losing his entire rearguard and supplies, including many of his most reputed knights.

The debacle in the Pyrenees inspired *La Chanson de Roland*, an epic poem of roughly 4,000 lines usually dated to around 1080. A version of it, however, was apparently sung to William the Conqueror's troops in 1066 to encourage them before their invasion of England. In the *Chanson*, Roland is Charlemagne's nephew and one of twelve *pairs* – commanders – of a rearguard of 20,000 men, beset by an ambush of 100,000 Saracens. Roland's honour dictates that he may not sound his horn to call back his uncle's main force and, when the rearguard finally repels the ambush, only 300 Franks have survived. Roland at last sounds his horn – not to summon assistance, but in the hope that Charlemagne will return to bury their bodies and avenge their deaths. Although unharmed by any weapon, Roland blows so hard that he ruptures 'the temple of his head' and bleeds to death.

The disastrous Spanish campaign probably inspired – from some Dark Ages spin doctor – the glorious and conciliatory legend of the naming of the fortified city of Carcassonne. The most famous version comes from the middle of the 19th century and is told by Gaston Blanchot de Brénas, a magistrate and storyteller from Lyon. He claimed to have heard it direct from one of the Cité's oldest inhabitants:

The Holy Emperor Charlemagne was determined to wrest the stronghold of Carcassonne from the Saracens and dedicate it to Christ, son of God, omnipotent master. In company with his 12 *pairs* and 1,200 paladins, with an innumerable escort of soldiery, he swept down from the neighbouring mountains like a sea in flood.

Master of the fortress was Prince Balaak. He gathered his Arab knights and told them: 'The thicker the harvest, the more joy to the harvester. By Allah's will, my brothers, our harvest shall be great.' But in the first skirmish the Prince was killed with most of his knights and the joy was in the tents of the Christians and the tears and the mourning in the Cité.

Balaak's widow, however, the virtuous and valiant Carcas, decked herself in her husband's armour and placed herself at the head of her remaining knights. From this point, Charlemagne's victories became rarer and the siege stretched out five long years.

The fighting in the field and the lists was picturesque and honourable. Great and deadly blows were struck but always with courtesy and nobility. Charlemagne admired Carcas. The Emperor's favourite, Count Oliban, carrying

Today, a carving of Dame Carcas looks out over the entrance to the Cité.

on his cheek a scar from her blade, loved her devotedly.

There came an evening after a day of fierce combat when Carcas re-entered the Cité alone but for her dwarf and her page. On the first day of the sixth year of the siege, both were dead. So Carcas had her soldiers make straw men to stand in the crenellations of the battlements. Charlemagne was dismayed: 'It is a miracle that so many defenders remain on the Cité walls.' And he sighed.

The next day, Carcas discovered from her quartermaster that all the food that remained within the walls was a single pig and a skinful of wheat. She gave the wheat to the pig and, when it had eaten every grain, she took it up on to the walls and hurled it down at the feet of the Emperor. The animal split open and the grains of wheat spilled out from its ruptured stomach on the ground.

Seeing this, the Christians lost heart: 'They have so much to eat they give the best grain to their animals.' Charlemagne gathered his 12 *pairs* and his 1,200 paladins and ordered them to lift the siege. The army formed line and began to troop away from the magnificent walls. At the rear, Charlemagne rode with Oliban, who turned to gaze behind him with regret at every second stride.

Then, all at once, the trumpet of a herald sounded from the battlements. Emperor and Count spun round to observe the great tall Tour Pinte bow its head in two honourable genuflections to its rightful master, raising its roof like a hat.

Count Oliban was delighted: '*Carcas sonne!*' he shouted. 'Carcas sounds the trump!' The Emperor was no less pleased. 'A joyful name indeed! Henceforth Carcassonne shall be the name of the Cité, and I make it yours to rule. I also desire that you should marry the Lady who has shown herself worthy of a Christian marriage with a Christian nobleman.'

The Emperor's wishes were fulfilled and Oliban and Carcas were happy and had many children, founding a long dynasty of noble counts.

In the 12th-century donjon of the Château Comtal in Carcassonne, there is a fresco depicting a battle between Franks and Saracens, as well as a bust of Dame Carcas carved in stone in the 16th or 17th centuries in the Lapidary Museum. (The bust exhibited out of doors at the Porte Narbonnaise is a copy.)

As his reign progressed, Charlemagne's forces captured Corsica, Sardinia and the Balearic Islands. He received an Asian elephant and a mechanical clock containing a toy bird that chirped the hours in tribute from the caliph of Baghdad. Decisively for the history of the entire continent of Europe, he was called on a second time to come to the aid of the pope.

Pope Leo III had been deposed by the people of Rome, who threatened to put out his eyes and pull out his tongue. The devout Charlemagne subdued the rebellion and attended a council in the Holy City on 1 December 800. Leo swore an oath of innocence and, on Christmas Day, he crowned Charlemagne *Imperator Romanorum* – 'Emperor of the Romans' – in the basilica of St Peter. Einhard claims that Charlemagne 'at first had such an aversion that he declared that he would not have set foot in the church … if he could have foreseen the design of the Pope'.

The issue was one of power and diplomacy. In rival Constantinople, there was already an *Imperator Romanorum*. Pope Leo believed he could increase the influence of the Latin papacy by sponsoring Charlemagne, at the same time as taking himself out of the legal sphere of influence of the Greek-speaking imperial families of the Eastern Empire. Leo wanted his own Holy Roman Emperor.

The emperor expired in 814 and was buried in the chapel at Aix-la-Chapelle, but not before making Louis the Pious, his only surviving son, his rightful heir. Einhard wrote: 'He died on 28 January, seven days after taking to his bed, at nine o'clock in the morning, having taken communion, in the seventy-second year of his age and the forty-seventh of his reign.'

The reliquary at Aix cathedral was supposed to contain a toenail of St Peter and a thigh bone of Charlemagne, alleged to have the ability – perhaps appropriately – to cure lameness. (The last Holy Roman Emperor to be crowned in Aix was Frederic I in 1536.)

The great empire lasted only one more generation as, according to tradition, the lands were divided between the sons of Louis the Pious, creating the divisions that would eventually result in the modern states of France and Germany. This accident of history – in other cultures, the throne might never have been divided but would have been inherited by the first-born male heir in its entirety – is also one reason why, in the 10th century, when the French line failed, the title of Holy Roman Emperor could only pass into the hands of the German line.

Authority across the great empire of Charlemagne moved north. The independence of the south – unknown since the time of the Celtic Volcae – reasserted itself. In the wide and fertile corridor of land that stretches from the vast and sandy estuary at Bordeaux to the lagoons and salt-marshes of the Golfe du Lion, in the years following Louis's death, history would at last see the emergence of the two great medieval families of Languedoc: Trencavel and Toulouse.

CHAPTER 8

Millennium

With the passing centuries, the Roman heritage reasserted itself in the West. Many of the so-called barbarians who had conquered the Western Roman Empire were Arian Christians. It was a small step for them to adopt the Roman Catholic beliefs of the people they had conquered, the better to manage taxes and tithes. Little by little they abandoned their tribal structures and adopted Roman law. Non-Christian tribes converted and, by the 9th and 10th centuries, the majority of central, western and northern Europe acknowledged the pope in Rome as the 'Vicar of Christ'.

But the turmoil hadn't ended. The millennium was approaching and the Christian world was seized by a frenzy of doom. Self-appointed prophets – most widespread in France, Germany and Italy – foretold the end of the world and the Last Judgment. They predicted a literal vision of Christ appearing in the clouds to judge the godly and the ungodly. The location for the appearance of Christ in Glory was generally thought to be Jerusalem.

Some priests did their best to discourage these fantasies but, in the months leading up to the end of the year 999 CE, many European Christians decided to sell all their property and travel to the Holy Land. Pilgrims of all classes – 'knights, citizens and serfs' – undertook the pilgrimage. They travelled together in nervous bands, singing psalms and praying. In fact, so many Christians decided to greet the Last Judgment in the Holy Land that their presence was likened to a 'desolating army'. They had nothing to live on but the money and valuables they carried with them, the proceeds of selling all their worldly goods before they left home.

The entire swollen Christian population of Jerusalem was repeatedly brought to its knees, weeping and praying, by a crack of thunder or the blink of a meteor or a shooting star. All across Europe, buildings and land were abandoned. Many of those who decided to remain at home did not bother to maintain their property. Here and there, market halls and other commercial buildings were pulled down in advance of Christ appearing and bringing judgment on the *banquiers* – money-changers and lenders.

The money-changers set up their scales on benches – bancs – *in market squares and were therefore known as* banquiers. *The English word 'banker' comes from this root.*

In the end, however, it turned out that the end of the world was not nigh. One after another, the catastrophic deadlines were passed. The oceans declined to boil. The sky remained bright in the daytime. The stars continued to turn at night. Each morning the sun shone, apparently having no alternative, on nothing new. Against many expectations, Christians survived to return to their humdrum concerns of survival and profit. Meanwhile, their church leaders lurched further and further towards schism.

Did the Holy Spirit proceed from God alone, or from God and Jesus? Who had authority over the churches in the Balkans, southern Italy and Sicily? What was the official title of the patriarch of Constantinople? Did the patriarch of Rome – the pope – have authority over the other patriarchs? What about the eastern patriarchs of Antioch, Jerusalem and Alexandria, weakened by the rise of Islam? Should Christians use leavened or unleavened bread in the Eucharist?

The endgame came unexpectedly in 1053–4. The Emperor Constantine IX in the East and Pope Leo IX – who was able to speak Greek – had been allies, but they came into conflict through an increasingly bitter dispute over control of regional churches, conducted through hot-headed emissaries, known as legates.

Leo died on 19 April. Three months later, three of his legates – whose authority should in truth have ended with his death – entered the church of the Hagia Sophia in Constantinople during mass and placed a papal bull of excommunication on the altar. The provocation was immediately followed by a tit-for-tat excommunication of the legates by Constantinople. The event led to riots in the Eastern capital.

Some say that ordinary Christians were largely unaware of the rift in their church. But, looking back, the timing of the schism coincides with a great European blossoming of religious communities, reassessing and redefining their spirituality and beliefs. Among them were the new ascetic orders, inspired by biblical 'rules' of poverty, chastity, manual labour and obedience. Others, like the Bogomils, rejected the entire material world, preaching a still more austere yet oddly tolerant Christianity.

Destined for fatal conflict were the white-cowled Cistercians of Bernard of Clairvaux, the Black Monks of St Dominic – the Dominicans – and the *Bons Chrétiens* themselves, the Cathars.

CHAPTER 9

Bogomils

*I*n the second half of the 10th century CE, in what we now call Bulgaria, a new church arose. Its members were called Bogomils. Shortly afterwards, certain monks of Constantinople and Asia Minor avowed the same faith. The established Christian church dismissed them as 'Manicheans', followers of the dualist philosophy of Mani, a Mesopotamian Christian born around 216 CE.

Mani claimed to be the 'other Paraclete' foretold by John's Gospel, 'the one who consoles', 'the one who intercedes on our behalf'. Mani believed that the world was an arena of combat between two balanced, opposing forces – good and evil, light and dark. Religions that see Creation in these terms are called dualist. Calling them dualists was supposed to be an insult, but it was, in fact, a good description.

The problem for this new church was that its faith made it independent of the pope. No sooner had it begun to take hold than it was condemned. Around 970 CE, a priest named Cosmas wrote what was probably the first theological treatise to denounce Christians similar in outlook and belief to the Cathars.

Cosmas wrote that 'Bogomil' meant 'lover of God' and was appalled that the Bogomils denied that Mary was the mother of 'God made flesh', believing that the incarnation was an illusion. He was aghast that the Bogomils denied the superstitious rituals of the church sacraments, that they dismissed the paraphernalia of belief – crosses, vestments, cups and plates. He was outraged to report that their only ritual was a baptism by the spirit through the 'laying on of hands'.

Bogomil priests travelled widely around the Mediterranean trying to convert people to their faith. In 1053, the Catholic church was split by schism. Caught between the rocks of the rift, the Bogomils dressed in black robes and let their beards and hair grow long. They believed that the world was created by the Devil and that the Word of God was only to be found in the New Testament, not the Old. Their faith grew to become the state religion in Bosnia and Serbia (until the Turks wiped it out in the 15th century). Their simple ritual of salvation was a blessing accompanied by the imposition of hands – or the Gospel – on the head of the supplicant.

Perhaps spontaneously, perhaps by evangelism, other groups similar to them sprang up in Burgundy, in Germany, in Flanders and in Champagne. While the Catholic church sold the sacraments – marriage, baptism, confession, last rites and masses for the dead – these ascetic Christians offered devotion and resignation. Substantial communities of believers took deep root in northern Italy and in the region of southwest France that we now call Languedoc.

Across the Continent, communities of Christians professed that their souls were created by God and had nothing but good in them. They believed that Satan had, by trickery, stolen their souls from Paradise and imprisoned them in 'tunics of flesh' on earth. In fact, Satan had created the Earth specifically as a prison for these souls. Christ – the 'first Paraclete' according to John's Gospel – was sent to Earth to awaken in these souls the memory of Heaven. Cosmas was correct. Neither the Bogomils nor the Cathars of Languedoc believed that Christ was God incarnated as man.

Bogomil belief came from a close reading of the Bible. They compared the God of the Old Testament – vengeful, punishing – with that of the New Testament – understanding, forgiving – and decided that they could not be the same being. The Old Testament stories of the Creation of the material world could only be descriptions of the work of Satan, the 'Prince of this world'. They decided that everything that they could see, hear, smell, taste and touch were the work of a 'bad creator'. After all, these things were corruptible; they could be seen to decay. It was, surely, absurd to suggest that anything created by God could decay. And they proclaimed that, as God was wholly good, He could not cause misery and pain. In fact, it was to deny the complete 'goodness' of God to suggest that He might use Satan's tools of suffering and misery: 'A good tree cannot bring forth bad fruit.'

The New Testament was different. It told the story of Christ, sent by God to remind the trapped souls of their true home at God's side. The Bogomils believed that Christ's role was to announce this 'good news'. In Languedoc, as the priest's hands or the New Testament were laid on the head of the believer in the baptism of consolation, the beginning of St John's

Gospel was recited: 'In the beginning was the Word, and the Word was with God, and the Word was God. The same was in the beginning with God.'

John's Gospel includes many references to pairs of opposing forces or qualities: light and dark, good and evil, truth and deception. It seems to fit very well with the dualist view that there are two Creations: the material world created by Satan as a prison for the souls stolen by trickery from Heaven; the spiritual world, God's Heaven, to which all souls are ultimately destined to return. And it is, first and foremost, the story of the life of Christ, whose revelation was later described by Jacques Authié, a Cathar priest from the early 14th century:

Someone came from God the Father and restored our memories and showed us with the Scripture He brought with him how we will regain salvation and escape from the power of Satan…And he came by the mouth of the Holy Spirit, He who showed us the way of salvation. He showed us also through the Scriptures that, just as we were exiled from Paradise by the trickery and pride of the devil, for having believed Satan rather than God, we must return to Heaven through humility, truth and faith.

CHAPTER 10
Languedoc

anguedoc is named for the language spoken there – it is the land of the *langue d'oc*. To the east is Provence and the old tongue of *provençal*, to the west, towards Perpignan and across the Pyrenees into Catalonia, is *catalán*. A little further and the people speak *castellano* – Spanish. In Toulouse there is a special brand of Occitan – *toulousain* – and a distinctive version of *provençal* in the Rhône valley.

The northerner who – perhaps with envy – put down his cup at midday and looked south to the sunny Midi spoke another language – not the *langue d'oc* but the *langue d'oïl*. He couldn't understand the jabbering of the Carcassonnais or the Pyrenean shepherd from a village in Aragon who spoke *catalán*, a *langue de sí*.

Oc, *oïl* and *sí*. What connects these three little words? The answer is that they each mean 'yes' in their respective tongues. They were first used to describe what language the scattered peoples spoke in the 12th century, but the most famous explanation comes from the 14th century and the Italian poet Dante. Writing in medieval Latin, he said: 'Some say *oc*, some say *oïl* and some say *sí*.'

The three versions of the word for 'yes' all seem to come from the language of Rome. In conversational medieval Latin, a common expression signifying agreement was *hoc ille*, meaning, literally, 'this it'. It seems that this was contracted in different ways by the different peoples, some choosing to say *oc* from the root *hoc*, the others saying *oïl* from the root *ille*. Another way of saying, in Latin, that you agreed was to use the word *sic*, meaning 'thus'. From this root came the languages Dante referred to as the *langues de sí*, like Spanish (*sí*), Italian (*sì*) or Portuguese (*sim*). (Although, in the Middle Ages, *oïl* was almost certainly pronounced with a strong *l*, today it is conventional to say it like the modern French word for 'yes', as if it was the *langue d'oui*.)

The classic pattern for building a medieval village or town in Languedoc was to create a *castrum* – a kind of common fortification made up of the dwellings themselves. It was the same in Italy, where the process was called *incastellamento* – 'encastlement'. The houses were grouped round a central square and sometimes arranged in concentric rings – a *circulade*.

Even today, the circulade *construction of Bram is still clearly visible.*

The strongest *castra* were built on high ground and the houses became part of the natural defensive position. Here and there, the *castrum* encircled a tower or a small *château*, but almost always there was that important public space. In those towns and villages in which Cathars lived openly – Laurac, Le Mas-Saintes-Puelles, Fanjeaux and so many others – they could be seen carding, weaving and spinning, reciting their prayers, fasting, receiving the faithful.

In tourist guides to Languedoc, they call the spectacular *châteaux* of the mountains – Montségur, Peyrepertuse, Quéribus – 'Cathar castles'. But these are just the places that provided their last desperate refuge, the austere peaks where many of them died. The town and village *castra* of the lowlands are the only real 'Cathar castles', the fortified public spaces where they lived.

And in many of these villages and towns, the central space where life was shared has been squatted by a great thickset Norman interloper: in the public square where goods and gossip and children's play should dominate, there is now a church.

The importance of the *castra* came from the fact that power in medieval France was local, based on a complex web of feudal allegiances.

Feudalism is a way of organising society. It evolved in France when the empire of Charlemagne began to fall apart, the vast inheritance split between his grandchildren. In place of the one supreme lord came a set-up in which each local lord had authority over his own lands and could pass on that authority to his children and grandchildren. (In Languedoc, power could be and was passed down to female children too.)

Alongside these inherited prerogatives came rights and responsibilities and a ladder of power with carefully defined steps. Each and every landowner could look down on those beneath them and up to those with more power. Looking up, obedience and material homage were due. Looking down, military support and political protection were owed.

The *comté* of Toulouse – including a large stretch of land along the Rhône valley – was created by Charlemagne himself in 778. In the feudal pyramid, the count of Toulouse was supposed to answer to the French king's representative in the west-coast kingdom of Aquitaine, but the prosperity of the south made it indifferent to outside events. That said, Toulouse had close links of fealty to the kingdom of Aragon on the southern side of the Pyrenees in modern Spain.

One of the great cities of Languedoc was Albi, known as the *ville rouge* for the red stone used in the construction of many of its older buildings, including a vast cathedral. It is in the French *département* of the Tarn, on a long meander in the river of the same name, about 70 kilometres due northeast of the *ville rose* – Toulouse. Some say its lack of contemporary dynamism comes from being a dormitory town for the industrial and academic hotspot of the *ville rose*. Its name in *langue d'oc* is the same as in modern French.

The Trencavel dynasty was founded around 840 CE, just a couple of generations after the death of Charlemagne, by Aton, viscount of Albi. Among his descendants, the traditional family names began mesmerically to repeat. As the millennial Catholic church began to burn Cathar 'heretics', around 1010 to 1060 CE, the Trencavels acquired the viscounty of Nîmes by marriage. (The best guess for the origin of the name seems to come from '*avelana*' – 'hazelnut' – and '*trenca*' – 'cut' or 'break'.) The house prospered under Aton II and Bernard-Aton III and then – crucially – Raymond-Bernard Trencavel married Ermengarde of Carcassonne.

At the time, Carcassonne belonged to the house of Aragon, but not much had really been made of the impressive defensive position occupied by the hill. In 1082, their son, Bernard-Aton IV, decided to occupy the Cité and, finding that the house of Aragon failed to react, he established a power base there. He also married Cécile of Provence and extended the domains of the house of Trencavel to viscount of Albi, Agde, Carcassonne, Nîmes, Razès and Béziers.

There were probably about twenty-five or thirty towers circling the summit of the hill. The walled suburbs of Saint-Michel and Saint-Vincent extended the fortifications northeast and southeast. The Cité became increasingly prosperous as control of the roads north and south through the Carcassonne gap made it possible for the family to tax travelling merchants severely. In 1096, Pope Urban II blessed the building materials made ready for the construction of the impressive cathedral of Saint-Nazaire.

Then Urban turned his attention to Jerusalem and the Crusader wars began.

⚏ CHAPTER 11 ⚏
The First Crusade

*I*n 1095 CE, everyone knew that Christ had told his followers: 'Love thy neighbour as thyself.' Then Pope Urban II changed the rules:

*Y*ou must hasten to carry aid to your brethren dwelling in the East . . . For the Turks, a Persian people, have attacked them…Wherefore with earnest prayer I – not I but God exhorts you as heralds of Christ to repeatedly urge men of all ranks whatsoever…to hasten to exterminate this vile race from our lands.

After the Muslim conquest of Jerusalem in 637 CE, for years a limited religious coexistence was maintained. Then, in 1009, the unpredictable Caliph Hakim began to persecute Christians and Jews. He ordered the destruction of churches and synagogues, including the church of the Holy Sepulchre. He executed his own officials, prohibited certain traditional recipes and made chess illegal. He is alleged to have punished fraudulent traders by allowing one of his slaves to sodomise them.

News of Hakim's persecutions found their way to Constantinople and Rome, without provoking an armed response. Meanwhile, a dynasty of Muslim Turks founded by Seljuk conquered lands from the Aegean Sea to Central Asia, displacing the Arab Muslim leaders. In 1071, at the Battle of Manzikert in Armenia, they crushed the forces of the Byzantine emperor, who was captured and ransomed. There were reports that Christian pilgrims travelling to Jerusalem were being abused or racketeered. In 1074, Pope Gregory VII in Rome vainly called for 'soldiers of Christ' to go to the aid of their Eastern brothers, but the call was ignored or opposed.

Finally, more than 2,000 years after the death of King David, came the invasion that provoked Urban's call to arms. The Seljuks conquered Jerusalem and began to turn away Christian pilgrims, denying them access to their holiest shrines. At first, the response was muted. Then, Alexios I Komnenos, the new Byzantine emperor of Constantinople, leader of the church in the East, swallowed his diplomatic pride and called on Pope Urban II in Rome for assistance. For a while the schism in the Christian world became less important than fighting a common enemy.

Urban had to 'sell' his Crusade for religious conquest in a crowded marketplace. At the time, the concept of a 'Crusader' was fairly new and they were simply known as 'pilgrims'. But the idea and practice of a religious war was already common currency. The Normans were fighting the Arab Muslims for control of Sicily, while Pisa, Genoa and Aragon were all battling Islamic strongholds in Mallorca and Sardinia to end the threat of Muslim raids on the coasts of Italy and Spain. Spanish knights, aided by European mercenaries, were engaged in a ramshackle campaign of *Reconquista* against the Moors in Spain.

At the Council of Clermont in central France, Urban preached an impassioned sermon. He told the assembled knights and clerics that the Holy Land was overflowing with milk and honey. He bemoaned the overcrowded population of France and suggested the obvious territorial solution. Taking part in the Crusade, he said, would 'let robbers become knights … For all those going thither there will be remission of sins.'

That meant that taking part in a Crusade, whatever the result of the campaign and whatever an individual's actions, would automatically grant the Crusader a complete and unquestioned absolution for any and all of the misdeeds of their lives. The audience received his words with enthusiasm, shouting: '*Deus vult!*' ('God wills it!')

The Christian Crusaders were inspired by a desire for plunder and conquest, but also by a dream of spiritual salvation. Many had been brought up in a culture that revered the Holy City. Perhaps they believed the prophesy that, at the Last Battle on the field of Armageddon, the Jerusalem Temple would rise up and the entire city would overspread the globe with towers and gardens, surrounded by seven walls of silver, gold, precious stones, lazulite, sapphire, emerald and fire. They would have known the medieval saying that 'Ten measures of beauty alighted upon the Earth. Nine were possessed by Jerusalem and the tenth was shared by the rest of the world.'

Urban tried to ensure that his Crusade was a proper military campaign and attempted to deny the right to women, to clerics and the sick. He chose 15 August 1096, the Feast of the Assumption, as the date for departure. But his words had created so much enthusiasm that the movement quickly escaped his control.

A monk named Peter the Hermit, from Amiens in northern France, set out with a People's Crusade of about 100,000, mostly civilian Crusaders. The army had no discipline and virtually no organisation. Still in Christian territory, they encountered huge problems of supply. Leaving several months early, in the spring, as the winter stocks were becoming exhausted, food was scarce and prices high. They became a mob and turned to looting. Attacked in turn, about a quarter of them died before they reached Constantinople in August.

There they met other groups from France and Italy, putting a huge strain on the capital of the Eastern Empire. The Byzantine emperor Alexios swiftly organised ferries to transport the army across the Bosphorus into Anatolia, where the army quarrelled and split into two. Both portions were decimated by the well-prepared and properly led Seljuks.

Urban's sermon at Clermont seemed, to many people, to promise reward for killing non-Christians of any sort. In early summer of 1096, around 10,000 Crusaders marched northwards up the valley of the Rhine – away from Jerusalem – towards well-known Jewish communities such as Cologne. The Jews were given a choice of conversion or death and – despite the protection of some local Christians – many were slaughtered.

Finally, a well-ordered army set out for Jerusalem, including Raymond IV of Toulouse, Robert of Normandy, the elder brother of King William II of England, and Hugh of Vermandois, younger brother of King Philip I of France. Wisely, the army broke into sections and took different routes to Constantinople, easing the problems of supply. They arrived in Constantinople in December 1096.

There was instant discord. Alexios was suspicious of the Crusaders' motives and unwilling to provision them without an oath of fealty to his throne. Finally, a Byzantine army joined the Crusader force and the troops set out for Nicea. A lengthy and unsuccessful siege was concluded when Alexios's commander gave the city the option of surrender and Byzantine protection. The Crusaders awoke on the morning of 19 June 1097 to see the standard of Alexios flying on the walls and were forbidden to sack the city for their promised loot. Distrust between the Eastern and Western armies grew.

A sequence of – mostly successful – battles and skirmishes slowed their advance to a crawl. The heat of summer 1097 killed many men and horses. Resupply was available only by pillage with none of the gifts of food and drink they had received while still in Christian Europe. Military leadership was disputed. Baldwin of Boulogne took an independent force to overthrow Edessa, where he became count of the first Crusader state.

In October 1097, the main bulk of the army attempted to besiege Antioch, about midway between Constantinople and Jerusalem. The Crusaders were too few to enforce a proper blockade and the siege dragged on for eight months. In May 1098, Muslim reinforcements were approaching. The anonymous contemporary chronicle known as the *Gesta Francorum* – the Deeds of the Franks – says: 'The Turks pressed us on all sides, so that none of us dared now to go out of the tents, for they constrained us on one side, and excruciating hunger on the other; but of succour and help we had none.'

Bohemund, a Norman Crusader, bribed an Armenian guard, who traitorously surrendered two or three defensive towers. The Crusaders entered the walls and slaughtered the inhabitants. They were swiftly besieged in their turn by the Muslim reinforcements. An insignificant monk named Peter Bartholomew claimed to discover the Holy Lance with which Christ's side was pierced and the Crusaders rejoiced at this favourable sign. They entered into a pitched battle outside the walls. Legend tells that an army of Christian saints marched alongside them.

Bohemund claimed the city of Antioch and, as Alexios had suspected, denied his oath of fealty to Constantinople. A year of squabbling between the leaders of the Crusade was made worse by an outbreak of some plague – perhaps typhoid or highly virulent dysentery – which killed, among many others, the papal legate. The lesser knights threatened to continue to Jerusalem without their lords and a hasty compromise saw Bohemund left behind as first prince of Antioch.

Peter Bartholomew died after attempting to prove the authenticity of the Holy Lance with an ordeal by fire. Nevertheless, without their talisman, the journey down the eastern end of the Mediterranean was easier because the local rulers preferred to cooperate, following the example of the king of Tripoli who:

From Toulouse, the distance by land to Jerusalem is over 3000 miles.

*m*ade an agreement with the leaders, and he straightway loosed to them more than three hundred pilgrims who had been captured there and gave fifteen thousand *besants* and fifteen horses of great value; he likewise gave us a great market of horses, asses and all goods, whence the whole army of Christ was greatly enriched. But he made an agreement with them that if they could win the war...and could take Jerusalem, he would become a Christian.

When the Crusader army reached Jerusalem on 7 May 1099, many wept with spiritual joy and physical relief. Perhaps only 1,500 of the original 7,000 Christian knights remained. The king of Tripoli was right to fear the self-righteous ferocity of the 'soldiers of Christ'.

▣ CHAPTER 12 ▣

Slaughter in the Temple

edieval warfare was a process of attrition, comprised of sequences of tactical withdrawals, stand-offs and sieges, punctuated by brief episodes of ferocity, barbarity and vengeance. Many of those who fought on the side of the Catholic church in Palestine became inured to carnage, schooled in contempt for 'heretics'. They would soon bring these unhappy attributes to bear on the people of Languedoc.

The majority of those who travelled to the Holy Land were illiterate. Both the Arab Muslims and the Seljuk Turks used the crescent moon as their emblem. In all the years of crusading, many of the Christians never seem to have fully grasped that these were separate Muslim peoples with their own internecine conflicts. In fact, while the Crusaders were on the long march east, possession of the Holy City changed Muslim hands.

Another siege was soon under way. Food and water were scarce. The walls of Jerusalem were impressively high – as were Crusader casualties. Inspired by the biblical story of Joshua – but without the assistance of the power of the Ark – a priest named Peter Desiderius announced that a divine vision had instructed him that the city would fall in nine days if the army agreed to fast and then march barefoot round the walls. On 8 July 1099, the Crusaders followed his instructions. More crucially, the commander of the Genoese troops had his men break up their ships and use the wood to build siege towers and pull down sections of the fortifications. Swiftly, on 15 July, the Crusaders entered the city.

Many Muslims sought sanctuary in the Temple of Solomon, today the site of the al-Aqsa mosque:

*O*ne of our knights, named Lethold, clambered up the wall of the city, and no sooner had he ascended than the defenders fled from the walls and through the city. Our men followed, killing and slaying even to the Temple of Solomon, where the slaughter was so great that our men waded in blood up to their ankles…Afterward, the army scattered throughout the city and took possession of the gold and silver, the horses and mules, and the houses filled with goods of all kinds.

The Crusaders made their way to the church of the Holy Sepulchre to fulfil one of their vows to worship there. According to Fulcher of Chartres, chaplain to Baldwin, the new count of Edessa, 'None of them was left alive; neither women nor children were spared.' Perhaps some Crusader lords attempted to mitigate the slaughter. Perhaps records of the massacre are exaggerated. In any case, the *Gesta Francorum* says of the dead: 'No one knows their number except God alone.' The same pious knights who prayed at the Sepulchre then crept on to the roof of the Temple where some Muslims were hiding and beheaded them with 'naked swords'. Some of their victims leapt from the roof.

Godfrey of Bouillon refused to take the crown of Jerusalem where Christ had worn a 'crown of thorns' so was styled 'Protector of the Holy Sepulchre'. He soon died in July 1100 and was succeeded by his brother Baldwin of Edessa, who had no such qualms, though his court numbered no more than a few hundred knights.

Many Crusaders had died but many, too, had returned home well before reaching Jerusalem. When word of the success of the Crusade reached western Europe, the deserters were mocked and even threatened with excommunication. After all, they had taken vows which amounted to an affirmation of two simultaneous medieval ideals, that of holy warrior and holy pilgrim. So, in 1101, a new baronial expedition set out, once more to fight their way through Seljuk territory and reinforce the garrison of the Holy City. They were not the last.

In 1108, Hugh of Payens visited Jerusalem with his liege lord, the count of Champagne. Hugh of Payens was a veteran of Godfrey of Bouillon's forces on the original Crusade. His purpose, with two of his brothers and six other male relatives, was to ask King Baldwin permission to form an order of fighting monks to protect pilgrims on the road between Jerusalem and Jaffa. The Cistercian Bernard of Clairvaux devised a 'rule' for the warrior monks, including a vow of poverty, so the nine knights lived on charity and were known as the Poor Knights of Christ. Then King Baldwin allotted them quarters on Mount Moriah on the site of the ruined Temple of Solomon. The name of the order changed to the Poor Knights of Christ and the Temple of Solomon.

Today, finally, we call them the Knights Templar.

CHAPTER 13

Bernard of Clairvaux

Bernard of Clairvaux preaching the Second Crusade in the presence of King Louis VII.

In the early years of European Christianity, the monasteries of western and northern Europe relaxed the severe rules inherited from the East until there was really nothing very distinctive about the devoted worshipper's life at all. Then, in about 480 CE, the father of modern monasticism was born in Nursia in Umbria. His name was Benedict and he devised the 'rule' for monastic life on which all subsequent Western 'rules' were based – poverty, chastity, manual labour.

The years turned and the churches prospered. Some Christians discovered that their wealth sat poorly with their avowed ideals. A thousand years ago, many Christians looked forward to the Apocalypse. It was, after all, necessary so that the Second Coming might follow. Ralph Glaber, who despite his modern-sounding name lived around the turn of the first millennium, wrote:

As love waxed cold and iniquity abounded among mankind, perilous times were at hand for men's souls…For whenever religion has failed among the pontiffs, and strictness of the Rule has decayed among the abbots, and therewith the vigour of monastic discipline has grown cold, and by their example the rest of the people are become prevaricators of God's commandments, what then can we think but that the whole human race, root and branch, is sliding willingly down again into the gulf of primeval chaos?

The ancient Christian tradition of self-sacrifice reasserted itself, of devotion to God and withdrawal from secular society, inspired by Bible stories of hermits and holy men who lived lives of breathtaking deprivation and poverty.

During the reign of Pope Gregory VII, from 1073 to 1085, the Catholic church tried to recapture the moral high ground. A set of reforms was put in place that harked back to the example of Benedict. More significantly, the reforms were the first important steps in freeing the pope and his hierarchy from secular control – in other words, making the Catholic church completely independent of kings, princes and even the law.

The Gregorian reforms had to be carried out without losing the people, the church congregations that paid tithes and other tributes like 'first fruits' into the Catholic coffers. Other Christian groups, like the Cathars, were setting a more austere example. Monasteries were often places of pilgrimage themselves or were built on pilgrim routes. This – in addition to gifts from the families of wealthy young men who joined them – made them rich. The monks at Cluny, for example, were managers of other men's work and professional choristers who lived in a richly decorated and endowed abbey church.

In 1075, a monk named Robert left Cluny for Molesme and made his first attempt at living by the austere rule of Benedict in 'poverty, chastity and manual labour'. It was an immediate success. Robert and his brother monks swiftly developed a reputation for sanctity and began to attract substantial donations from wealthy, pious benefactors. Frustrated, in 1098, Robert moved on to Cîteaux, attempting to begin again.

Pope Urban II was impressed with the harsh rule by which the Cistercian monks lived, but he was dismayed that, in Robert's absence, the community at Molesme went into decline. He ordered Robert to return and the Cîteaux order strove on in poverty without him.

Contemporary observers believed the Cistercians were doomed. They received little assistance from the nobility in Burgundy. The abbots who succeeded Robert were scholars, not evangelists. For several years there had been no new novices. However, in 1113, Bernard of Fontaines-les-Dijon joined the order and everything changed.

Bernard came from a noble Burgundian family and was a charismatic and persuasive young man. (He was also reputed to be terrified of women. As an adolescent, experiencing sexual desire, he jumped into a freezing-cold pond and stayed there until his erection subsided.) Bernard convinced thirty-five of his relatives and friends to join him at Cîteaux.

More remarkably still, three years later Bernard was inspired to establish his own monastery in the freshly minted Cistercian tradition. To do this, he was granted land in the domains of the count of Champagne. He and twelve brother monks took possession of the Valley of Wormwood and renamed it the Valley of Light – Clairvaux. Bernard's leadership was extraordinarily successful. In 1118, there were fewer than ten Cistercian abbeys; by 1152 there were 328; by the end of the 12th century there were more than 1,200.

Meanwhile, Bernard was engaged by the Catholic church on missions of diplomacy, travelling through much of western Europe. His preaching, his emaciated ascetic appearance and his simple clothing made him stand out from the ostentatious and wealthy Catholic priesthood. Like Ralph Glaber 150 years earlier, Bernard believed that deviations from Catholic dogma were evidence of impending Apocalypse. But the apparently immutable date of destruction had long passed and, unlike Glaber, Bernard thought that disaster could be averted. He said the 'heretics' should be converted or, failing conversion, punished. This was God's work, striving more fully to establish His kingdom on Earth.

Bernard lent his considerable clout to ensuring the support of the pope in establishing the soldier monk order housed in the ruins of the Temple of Solomon in Jerusalem. He preached the disastrous Second Crusade to the Holy City. And he gave his spiritual authority to the genocidal war against the Cathars and the lords of Languedoc, known to history as the Albigensian Crusade.

CHAPTER 14
The Knights Templar

The Poor Knights of Christ and the Temple of Solomon were named for the quarters allotted to them by Baldwin, the second Crusader king of Jerusalem – the old threshing floor on Mount Moriah that King David set aside for the building of his son Solomon's temple. The medieval chronicler William of Tyre puts the foundation of the order at 1118. He was writing in the 1170s, when the Templar story had already become common currency:

Certain noble men of knightly rank, religious men, devoted to God and fearing him, bound themselves to Christ's service in the hands of the Lord Patriarch. They promised to live in perpetuity as regular canons, without possessions, under vows of chastity and obedience. Their foremost leaders were the venerable Hugh of Payens and Geoffrey of St Omer…The Lord King and his noblemen and also the Lord Patriarch and the prelates of the church gave them benefices from their domains, some for a limited time and some in perpetuity…to provide the knights with food and clothing. Their primary duty…was that of protecting the roads and routes against the attacks of robbers and brigands. This they did especially in order to safeguard pilgrims.

The 'certain noble men of knightly rank' included two of Hugh's brothers and seven other relatives by blood or marriage. As always, the question of a monastic rule and an appropriate habit or uniform became important:

*T*he knights wore secular clothing. They used such garments as the people, for their soul's salvation, gave them. In their ninth year there was held in France, at Troyes, a council at which the Lord Archbishops of Reims and Sens and their suffragans were present, as well as the Bishop of Albano, who was the legate of the apostolic see, and the Abbots of Cîteaux, Clairvaux, Pontigny, with many others. This council, by command of the Lord Pope Honorius and the Lord Stephen, Patriarch of Jerusalem, established a rule for the knights and assigned them a white habit.

Hugh had originally travelled to Jerusalem in 1099 with the First Crusade and possessed a certain amount of kudos on the strength of it. When he returned to the Holy City in 1108, it was in company with his liege lord, the count of Champagne. By 1127 Hugh and his knights had grown in influence but were not without opposition. King Baldwin II of Jerusalem sent him to Europe as his personal emissary and Hugh took advantage of the voyage to canvas support. He wrote to Bernard of Clairvaux, the leader of the most influential and dynamic monastic order in Europe, the Cistercians. There was a close feudal connection as Bernard and his brother monks had built their monastery at Clairvaux on lands gifted by the count of Champagne. And, of course, the council at Troyes took place in the lands of Champagne to the east of Paris.

Hugh requested Bernard's assistance in drawing up a 'rule' for the Templar order and, as an extension of this commitment, diplomatic or political help in gaining official recognition for the order within the Roman Catholic church. Between them they would have to overcome opposition, including some who pointed out that Christ had preached not violence but peace. The Templars were – unashamedly and by their vocation as defenders of pilgrims – soldiers. Bernard argued that Hugh of Payens' order could combine monastic virtue with military excellence:

*G*o forward in safety, knights, and with undaunted souls drive off the enemies of the cross of Christ, certain that neither death nor life can separate you from the love of God…repeating to yourself at every peril: 'Whether we live or whether we die, we are the Lord's.'…Life indeed is fruitful and victory glorious, but…death is better than either of these things. For if those are blessed who die *in* the Lord, how much more blessed are those who die *for* the Lord?

In 1128, official recognition was forthcoming and the order began to receive substantial donations of money and land from pious admirers. Crucially, the protection and patronage of the pope included exemption from paying church tithes. It also freed them from the threat of spiritual punishments such as excommunication. William of Tyre takes up the story:

lthough the knights now had been established for nine years, there were still only nine of them. From this time onward their numbers began to grow and their possessions began to multiply. Later...both the knights and their humbler servants...began to affix crosses made of red cloth to their mantles, so as to distinguish themselves from others.

The mantles to which the red crosses were affixed were, of course, white like the habits of the Cistercians. The order was made up of knights, equipped as medieval heavy cavalry, sergeants who made up the light cavalry, two grades of pages and other non-fighting men, farmers, other tradesmen and chaplains. They were wealthy and organised enough to build a substantial castle at Safèd in 1140 and Karak in 1143, whose ruins can still be seen today. The Templar model was followed by other orders of warrior monks who sought the same exemptions from church taxes. In 1156, the Christian clergy of the Holy Land tried to rein in their privileges. But the authority of the Templars, especially, was founded on their success as protectors of pilgrims and 'hammer of the Mohammedans'. If defeated and taken prisoner, the Templars refused to renounce Christianity and their order forbade the paying of ransoms. Many died as martyrs, their reputation for bravery undiminished.

In 1175, Usamah, a Muslim warrior and courtier who fought against the Crusaders with Saladin, the Muslim leader, wrote an autobiography. As well as fighting the men he called the 'Franks', he became friends with a certain number of Crusaders, but his opinion of their virtues was seriously limited:

ysterious are the works of the Creator, the author of all things! When one comes to recount cases regarding the Franks, he cannot but glorify Allah (exalted is he!) and sanctify him, for he sees them as animals possessing the virtues of courage and fighting, but nothing else; just as animals have only the virtues of strength and carrying loads.

In France, the Templars subdivided into eleven administrative areas, or bailiwicks. In turn, the bailiwicks comprised more than forty-two commanderies. One of the best preserved is at Sainte-Eulalie de Cernon, a village in the Aveyron in the north of Cathar Languedoc. In Paris in 1140, the French king Louis VII gave them a stretch of swampland in the north of the city. They drained the ground, put in substantial foundations and built a large square fortified tower and a characteristic round Templar chapel. The neighbourhood is known today as the *quartier du Temple*.

The turret on the corner of the Templar fort at Sainte-Eulalie is an échauguette - *a watch tower. It has been recently repaired.*

As the organisation grew in numbers and wealth, it became more irksomely independent of the Catholic church, its early sponsor. In the early 1170s, William of Tyre wrote:

They have now grown so great that there are in this Order today about 300 knights who wear white mantles, in addition to the brothers, who are almost countless. They are said to have immense possessions both here and overseas, so that there is now not a province in the Christian world which has not bestowed upon the aforesaid brothers a portion of its goods. It is said today that their wealth is equal to the treasures of kings...Although they maintained their establishment honourably for a long time and fulfilled their vocation with sufficient prudence, later, because of the neglect of humility (which is known as the guardian of all virtues and which, since it sits in the lowest place, cannot fall), they withdrew from the Patriarch of Jerusalem, by whom their Order was founded and from whom they received their first benefices and to whom they denied the obedience which their predecessors rendered. They have also taken away tithes and first fruits from God's churches, have disturbed their possessions, and have made themselves exceedingly troublesome.

At the same time as being 'exceedingly troublesome', the Templars and their 'countless' brothers had discipline and a sense of shared purpose that the original Crusader armies had lacked – 'the first to attack, the last to retreat'. They also invented the concept of a letter of credit which pilgrims could carry from place to place rather than purses of tempting cash. The pilgrim could make a deposit at a Templar commandery at the start of his or her journey, then redeem it from brother knights along the route. The Templars recycled the profits from these and other ventures in land and real estate in Europe and the Crusader states. At their height, they ran a large fleet of ships throughout the Mediterranean and even owned the island of Cyprus.

The Templars' bravery in battle – and the ensuing loss of life – made it difficult for the order to substantially increase the number of fully fledged knights. (One account says that there were never more than 400 knights in the Holy Land, even at the order's zenith, perhaps accompanied by some 3,000 sergeants.) In the order's original rule, a probationary period had to be fulfilled, but the thirst for new recruits meant that was abandoned and the order even began to accept excommunicated knights who wished to atone for their sins.

Those who sought to become members had to be of appropriate family lineage and nobility. They were obliged to submit to an initiation ceremony, which was always conducted in conditions of absolute secrecy. It was known to contain an oath to become 'servant and slave of the house' and, when political forces turned against the order, the secrecy of the Templar rituals was exploited as an opportunity for calumny and misrepresentation.

Did they excavate relics from the stables of the Temple? Did they bring them back in secret to their strongholds in France? There is no evidence that they did, except perhaps the fact of their ultimate persecution. The same combination of Catholic pope and French king that finally exterminated the Cathars would, eventually, mobilise to wipe out the Knights Templar too.

CHAPTER 15

The Book in Stone

Many people believe they have found early historical evidence of a pre-Christian sacred oak grove at the site of the Chartres cathedral. Possibly it was a place of druidical worship. It is said that Mary, mother of God, and Mary Magdalene fled to France accompanied by Joseph of Arimathea around 68 CE and visited the place. Christians probably arrived and settled or were converted in the area in the 4th century CE. The Christian place of worship here has been ruined many times. The first reference in history – to its destruction, for it seems somehow an unlucky place – was in 743 CE.

There is a well underneath Chartres cathedral. There are records that its water was considered miraculous from the 9th century on. (The cathedral clergy had it walled up in the 17th century but it was reopened in 1901.) In 876 CE, Charlemagne's grandson, Charles the Bald, is said to have presented the cathedral with a relic, the *sancta camisia*, the *chemise* or nightdress supposedly worn by the Virgin Mary whilst giving birth to Christ. In 911 CE, Chartres was besieged by a Viking chieftain named Rollon. Bishop Gantelmne displayed the *sancta camisia* on the city wall. Seeing this fragment of Mary's birthing gown, Rollon lifted the siege and converted to Christianity. Rollon was made duke of Normandy by King Charles III of France. William the Conqueror, who invaded England in 1066, was one of Rollon's descendants.

Chartres cathedral was the first of the great Gothic cathedrals of the Middle Ages to be dedicated to the Assumption of Our Lady, Mary, the first major European pilgrim site to celebrate the mother of God. (The Feast of the Assumption celebrates Mary's soul being borne up to Heaven three days after her death. Unlike Mary, who was drawn up, Christ is said to have 'ascended' – under his own steam as it were.) There are no tombs of any sort.

Fulbert was bishop of Chartres from 1007 to his death in 1028 CE. He was a leading scholar and political figure in northern France. The cathedral and its *quartier* became one of the great scholastic institutions of Europe. A flourishing stationery and book trade developed there. In 1020, the cathedral was once more badly damaged by fire and Fulbert contributed to its rebuilding, including part of the current crypt. Also in the 11th century, though perhaps later, the floor of the crypt was raised by about 1.2 metres. This ensured that only the clergy could have access to the cathedral's sanctuary, where its holy relics were kept. The high north tower of Chartres cathedral was completed in 1134. The south tower was added over the next two decades. The sloping floor of the nave in Chartres cathedral was designed to allow the water from pilgrims, washing themselves and their clothes, to drain away out of the great west door.

In 1194, a devastating fire again destroyed most of the city. (The *sancta camisia* – the cathedral's holiest relic – was saved by monks, who hid it in the crypt.) Funds were collected for rebuilding and the project clearly became a mission of great and widely held importance. Even though he was at war with Philip Augustus of France, Richard I of England – Richard the Lionheart – allowed English priests to collect and send money. It is said that the reconstruction was taken in hand and, to some extent, financed by the Knights Templar. In part, this story arises out of the odd fact that of all the medieval Gothic cathedrals, Chartres is the only one where the names of the master builders are unknown.

Because of its many esoteric sculptures and carvings, the cathedral has become known as the Book in Stone. In the north porch of Chartres cathedral – sometimes known as the Door of the Initiates – there is a stone pillar with an eerie procession of kings and queens of the Old Testament. Near the carving of the Queen of Sheba, there is a sculpture showing the Ark of the Covenant being loaded on to a donkey. Some say it shows the Ark being carried away from Jerusalem by Menelik, son of Solomon and the Queen of Sheba. Others claim the story of Menelik was unknown in Europe until the 15th century. Underneath the Ark and donkey is the inscription '*Hic amititur archa cederis*'. The Latin does not make complete sense. Perhaps it means that the Ark is being 'given up' – ceded. A more plausible text might read: '*Hic amicitur archa foederis*', meaning 'Here is let go the Ark of the Covenant'. Others have suggested 'You are to work through the Ark' or 'Here things take their course: you are to work through the Ark'.

Medieval Christians lived in a world in which the lives of the saints and readings from sacred works filled the place occupied today by theatre, cinema, books, music and the internet. Secular and folk literature flourished in local oral traditions, but written forms were restricted to a tiny elite. Art was the province of the wealthy. The countryside was unsafe, ravaged on a seemingly endless cycle by famine, fire, warfare, disease, thieves or a combination of all of these. Life in the cities was harsh, too. Much creative energy was channelled into religious life.

Cathedrals were the poor man's Bible. For us today, they are grey, speaking of sober devotion. But, in the Middle Ages, they were riotously colourful. The stained-glass windows of Chartres cathedral – designed to be read from left to right and from bottom to top – tell cinematic stories from the Bible. The walls and sculptures were gilded, the statues and tympana tricked out in polychrome, the naves smothered with frescos and decked with richly woven tapestries, eastern fabrics, silken banners all embroidered in gold. The skin of a sculpted saint was *really* pink, the robe of the Virgin Mary *really* blue. If you look carefully at the south porch, you can still see snatches of colour – pinks, blues, yellows – clinging tenaciously to the grooves in the stone.

Around 1200 CE, the stone labyrinth was laid in the floor of the nave. Today's visitor can still see the marks of the bolts that fixed an inscribed copper plate to the stone. It was removed in 1792 during the French Revolution and melted down. Contemporary records from eyewitnesses state that it showed Theseus, Ariadne and the Minotaur, all characters from Greek legend. The reliquary was also opened and much was lost in careless vandalism. A robe, 6.4 metres in length, was discovered and torn into six or seven pieces and scattered, believed irretrievably lost. More than a hundred years later, at the beginning of the 19th century, two pieces of the long robe were returned to the cathedral. Expert examination showed the cloth to be about 2,000 years old and of Near or Middle Eastern origin.

The pavement labyrinth at Chartres cathedral is a place of modern pilgrimage. Tourists from all over the world visit the cathedral, more or less well informed. Many of them leave the great Gothic building without ever having knowingly set eyes on the pavement labyrinth. It is often – in fact, almost always – covered by the chairs set out for cathedral services. This is, of course, contrary to its spirit and purpose.

The eleven-circuit labyrinth is also known as the *chemin de Jérusalem*. It is a representation of the journey undertaken by pilgrims to the Holy City. It is not a maze and it is not possible to take a wrong turning as there are no

junctions. There is one long and winding path into the centre and the only way out is to retrace one's steps. Walking the labyrinth should provide a means of duplicating – in miniature – the meditative, spiritually enlightening aspects of pilgrimage. Contemporary Templar rituals included symbolic journeys of pilgrimage, perhaps tramping seven times round a sarcophagus or altar table, on an imaginary *chemin de Jérusalem*.

The use of a labyrinth at Chartres was not unique. In the first century after Christ, Pliny the Elder wrote of four labyrinths in the ancient world – Cretan, Egyptian, Lemnian and Italian. There is a labyrinth very much like that of Chartres at the cathedral of San Martino in Lucca in Italy, but in miniature, carved on a wall. In 1288, the wonderful Gothic splendour of Amiens cathedral was adorned with its own labyrinth but, like Sens and St Omer, it seems to have been inspired by Chartres rather than originating with it.

During the Crusade against the Cathars, the pre-eminence of Chartres as a university city began to decline. (The University of Paris was founded in 1215.) But still money was available for the completion and decoration of the Book in Stone. Work was finally concluded around 1225. As Ken Follett says in *The Pillars of the Earth*:

*T*he building of the medieval cathedrals is an astonishing European phenomenon. The builders had no power tools, they did not understand the mathematics of structural engineering, and they were poor: the richest of princes did not live as well as, say, a prisoner in a modern jail. Yet they put up the most beautiful buildings that have ever existed, and they built them so well that they are still here, hundreds of years later, for us to study and marvel at.

⚏ CHAPTER 16 ⚏

Disasters in the East

*J*erusalem fell to the First Crusade in 1099, taken by a fraction of the force – or rather forces – that set out with such pomp and optimism from Europe. A kind of peaceful coexistence was established, then the fledgling Crusader state of Edessa was conquered by Muslim Turks and Bernard of Clairvaux preached a new Crusade to retake it.

An army of Franks and Germans set out in 1147. They were defeated at every important battle. They further endangered the fragile status quo with a reckless attack on the powerful Muslim stronghold of Damascus. Bernard wrote an *apologia* – a 'justification' – but he could not hide from the truth of the rout: 'The sons of the Church, those who bear the label "Christian", have been laid low in the desert and have either been slain by the sword or consumed by famine.'

While the Byzantine emperor in Constantinople extended the influence of the eastern Christian church, the Muslim leader Salah al-Din Yusuf, or Saladin, was busy establishing an empire of conquest in Egypt. New arrivals from the disastrous Second Crusade and other adventures found it hard to adjust to the *modus vivendi* in the disputed lands. The Europeans failed properly to unite and mistakenly assumed their own military superiority. A contemporary Muslim commentator shrewdly noted: 'Everyone who is a

Few representations of Saladin survive. This one can be seen in the British Library.

fresh emigrant from the Frankish lands is ruder in character than those who have become acclimatised and have held long association with the Muslims.'

In 1187, Saladin duly recaptured Jerusalem by siege. A Christian chronicler described the Muslim entrance into the city's holiest places: '...first to the Temple of the Lord...in which they have great faith for salvation. They believed they were cleansing it and with unclean and horrible bellows they defiled the Temple by shouting with polluted lips the Muslim precept: "*Allahu akbar! Allahu akbar!*" ' ('God is great!')

Saladin swiftly captured all the kingdom of Jerusalem and Pope Gregory VIII preached another Crusade, the Third. In Britain and France, Henry II and Philip II, also known as Philip Augustus, introduced a new tax – the Saladin tithe. Frederick I, the Holy Roman Emperor, owner of the crown first awarded to Charlemagne, set out in May 1189. The plan was to approach by sea across the Mediterranean, but his force was so vast he was obliged to march through Anatolia. On 10 June 1190, Frederick died while crossing the Saleph river in south-eastern Anatolia.

In Britain, Richard I – Richard the Lionheart – attacked and then succeeded his father, Henry II. Richard was Henry's third legitimate son and had been brought up in southwest France by his mother, Eleanor of Aquitaine. Richard could speak and write both *langue d'oc* and *langue d'oïl*. He was closely allied with Philip II of France, his half-brother, the son of Eleanor's ex-husband, Louis VII, by his third wife, Adèle of Champagne. They set out in July 1190 from Marseille, coming together once more at the siege of Acre in June 1191.

During the siege, an Englishman called Phillip of Mosse was given the right by King Richard I of England to bear arms, including the figure of a griffin sitting on a tower, meant to represent the defences of Acre. A Latin motto was later attached to the arms: '*Crux Christi Nobis Salus*' – 'the Cross of Christ Is Our Salvation'. Another Philip, the count of Flanders, patron of Chrétien of Troyes, also died at Acre. Chrétien was the author of *Li conte del Graal* – the very first story of the Grail – apparently inspired by a mysterious book provided by Philip of Flanders. No one knows if it ever really existed.

The victors of Acre began quarrelling among themselves over the spoils. Philip, the king of France, was in poor health and left the Holy Land in

August. Saladin reneged on the treaty of surrender and, in punishment, Richard executed some 3,000 Muslim prisoners in full view of Saladin's camp. On 2 September 1192, Richard and Saladin finalised a treaty by which Jerusalem would remain under Muslim control, but which also allowed unarmed Christian pilgrims to visit the city. That meant that the initial pretext for the First Crusade – that Christian pilgrims were being denied access to their holiest shrines in the Holy City – was no longer valid.

Saladin died in 1193 and, the following year, when the great fire devastated the city and cathedral of Chartres, Richard the Lionheart finally returned to England. For a short time the Crusades were over. But not for ever.

Pope Innocent III preached an ambitious Fourth Crusade in 1202, intending to retake Jerusalem by an attack through Egypt. Politics intervened. The powerful Venetians took control of the army and attacked the Christian city of Zara, then, in 1204, sacked the Eastern Orthodox capital, Constantinople. The war for control of the Holy Land seemed out of control. The Catholic church would soon turn its attention to a different target – more accessible, wealthier, closer to home.

The time had come for the overthrow of the political and religious independence of Languedoc.

CHAPTER 17

Pyres

*I*n the first half of the 11th century, 'heretics' were denounced in Champagne, Flanders, Aquitaine, Périgord and Toulouse. In Piedmont, in northern Italy, a community of 'heretics' was formed in a *castrum* called Monteforte. According to contemporary chronicles, the lady of the *castrum* was a believer and they practised a form of blessing of the ill and dying by laying on of hands. They were burnt in Turin in 1025. Other pyres were lit in Orléans and Toulouse.

As capital persecution became entrenched, Pope Gregory encouraged the growth of new monastic orders. In 1085, the king of Castile retook Toledo from the Muslim Moors and, in 1099, the First Crusade to the Holy Land captured Jerusalem. Around the same time, a Bogomil community led by Basil of Constantinople was burnt on a communal pyre because they claimed that only through their ritual of consolation could anyone be saved and that anyone who did not believe was

Here a medieval illuminated manuscript shows King Philip II of France presiding at the burning of the heretical followers of Amaury of Chartres.

under the influence of demons. Basil announced that the cross – the instrument of Christ's death – was a satanic symbol. He and his followers denied the teaching of all other Christian churches, including the primacy of the pope in Rome.

In the early 12th century, these ideas were becoming increasingly widespread. In response, more pyres were built – at Soissons in 1114 and, in the mid-1120s, for Peter of Bruys, who preached against infant baptism and taught that the cross should be hated since Christ died upon it. He denied any value in mass and argued for the demolition of churches because an omnipresent God had no need of them.

In the late 1130s in Liège, more pyres were lit for the first Cathar communities served by bishops. In 1143 in Cologne, human beings were again burnt alive. In the same year, a council of the Eastern church in Constantinople met to condemn those who said that Christ was 'merely an angel', or that Satan was the 'creator and ruler of the universe' or who refused to 'worship the cross'. A prior from the Rhine valley wrote to Bernard of Clairvaux for advice on how to combat the teachings of 'heretics', including a bishop who claimed to have knowledge of a secret tradition of salvation from ancient Greece.

Bernard was moved to action. He decided to travel south to Albi and Toulouse to speak out against heresy. He was met with disdain, the medieval equivalent of being booed off the stage. He was confronted by a community that appeared to accept Catharism as the default religion, a fact of life, unremarkable and comforting. It was run by priests that, later, the scribes of the Inquisition would call *perfecti* – 'perfected ones'. This is why French texts call them *parfaits* and *parfaites*. Among themselves, they referred to one another as Christians or Good Christians or, simply, Good Men and Women.

Unlike Catholic priests, Cathars would not sit on legal tribunals and refused to swear oaths because they refused under any circumstances to lie – so what was the point of an oath? (When interrogated by the Inquisition, their infallible honesty became a calamity for their colleagues and protectors.) They were celibate and refused to kill or eat any creature, human or animal, except for fish. They fasted regularly, eating only bread and water. Their communities respected them for their reliance on their own manual labour. Many worked as weavers. One of the last Cathar *parfaits*, Bélibaste, earned his living as a maker of combs. The people of Languedoc recognised the contrast with Catholics who preached poverty and lived in comfort by taxing the people.

Despite their ascetic lifestyle, Cathar priests were highly tolerant of the lives of their followers. (The Inquisition called them *credentes* – 'believers'.) Because Cathars rejected the idea of marriage as a church sacrament – how could the union of two bodies created by Satan have anything to do with God? – couples could separate simply by mutual consent. Unlike their Catholic neighbours, the Cathars did not consider themselves guilty of original sin. The travails of life in the material world created by Satan were not a judgment upon them. They knew that God was wholly good, incapable of doing or making anything bad. They knew that the evils of this world and everything in it – the sickness that carried off a loved child, the storm that destroyed the harvest – were created by Satan. Their only goal was to 'make a good end' and, on the death of their fleshly prison, return to Heaven. The only way for a Cathar to 'make a good end' was to die consoled, having received the *consolament* from a Cathar *parfait*.

If the Cathar died without being consoled, their soul was condemned to migrate to another body to begin again the search for a 'good end'. As well as being able to migrate to another human body, their souls could also be imprisoned in the body of an animal. (This is one of the reasons Cathar priests refused to eat meat.) If we fail to 'make a good end', there is no shame. Our soul must wait a little time and then return in a new body and seek salvation anew.

So Bernard's mission ended in ignominy and more pyres were lit and repression became more commonplace, especially in the Rhineland. Five Cathars were burnt in Cologne in 1163 – one of the five victims was a young girl. In 1165, a German monk called Eckbert von Schönau, the brother of the medieval mystic Elizabeth von Schönau, coined the term 'Cathar'. (Many sources say it was sixteen years later.) He said: '*Hos nostra germania catharos appellat*.' ('In Germany we call these people Cathars.')

The name 'Cathar' is a clever pun combining two pejorative meanings. Firstly, it was reminiscent of the 'catharists', an ancient Manichean sect, based on the Greek word for 'pure'. More unpleasantly, it called to mind 'catists', a way of referring to people accused of witchcraft and who were assumed to keep and worship cat familiars.

Both the Bogomils of the east and the Cathars of northern Italy had high-level contacts with the *Bons Chrétiens* of Languedoc. In 1167, the Bogomil bishop Nicetas and Bishop Marc of Lombardy came to a council at Saint-Félix-Lauragais and met the Cathar bishops of Albi, Toulouse, Carcassonne, Agen, Aran and France. Nicetas must have been envious of the support and faith given by the nobility of the southwest; in the east, the ruling classes saw the Bogomils as dangerous revolutionaries. Throughout the 12th century the term *'bougre'* – a corruption of 'Bulgar' – became synonymous at first with Bogomil, then, by extension to the supposed practices of sorcerers, with 'perverts' and 'sodomites'. *'Bougre'* was the origin of the modern insult 'bugger'.

In 1180, near Reims in Champagne, a young cleric of English origin groundlessly accused a young shepherdess who resisted his sexual advances. She was a Cathar and she was burnt. A few years later, again in Champagne, at Troyes, the Catholic chronicler Aubry of Trois-Fontaines tells of the burning of five men and three women – including 'two pitiful old maids'.

In 1187, Saladin retook Jerusalem. The Third Crusade forces of Philip Augustus of France, Richard the Lionheart of England and Frederic Barbarossa of Germany – launched with such pomp – failed to take it back. As the 12th century became the 13th, Italian Cathar bishoprics developed in at least six major cities, including Milan, Florence and Mantua. More Cathars were burnt in Nevers and in the Loire valley. In southwest France, it seems that some towns and villages were almost wholly inhabited by believers. It was normal, even mundane, to follow the *Bons Chrétiens*, to pray with them and ask their blessing.

For the pope in Rome, the affront of the success of Catharism would soon assume even more importance than the continuing debacle in the Holy Land. The first pyre of the Crusade against the Cathars took place at Casseneuil-en-Quercy in 1209. Guilhèm of Tudèla – author of the contemporary epic poem *The Song of the Crusade* – was amazed to find 'so many fine heretic ladies' among them. None could be in any doubt as to the horror and agony of such a death. Raimonde Jougla, a mid-13th-century Cathar believer who recanted, explained succinctly why: 'When they brought me to the pyre, through fear of the flames I converted to the Catholic faith.'

⊞ CHAPTER 18 ⊞

Beliefs

*B*élibaste, probably the last Cathar *parfait*, burnt by the Inquisition in 1321, said:

I care nothing for my flesh for there is nothing truly of me in it: it belongs to the worms…Likewise there is nothing of the Holy Father in my flesh and he does not wish it in his Kingdom, because human flesh belongs to he who made it, the Prince of this world. The Holy Father does not want anything made by the God and Prince of this world.

The logic of their position was hard to deny. The Catholic priest of Montaillou, Pierre Clergue, put it like this:

*G*od only made the souls. They are incorruptible and indestructible because the works of God last for eternity. But all things that can be seen or felt, like the sky, the Earth and all that is in it, only excepting the souls, these were made by the Devil, the Prince of this world.

For Cathars, the water that fell as rain and ran in streams down from the mountains of the Pyrenees was created by Satan. Because the 'Prince of this world' was wholly bad, everything that he created – the entire visible world – was also evil. So, for a Cathar, the idea that water could be 'holy' was a contradiction in terms. Pierre Authié, the most important Cathar *parfait* in the revival of the early 14th century, summed up the argument against baptism by water:

Baptism by the Roman Catholic church is worth nothing because it uses actual water and because utter lies are told in it. The child is asked: 'Do you want to be baptised?' and in its stead someone answers: 'Yes.' Meanwhile the child cries. Then they ask him if he believes this and that and people reply for him: 'Yes, he does.' But he doesn't believe anything yet, having not reached the age of reason.

He ironically dismissed the tradition of using so-called holy water to cross oneself:

*I*t's a good thing. In summer, it's a good way to get flies out of your face. As for the words [in the name of the Father, the Son and of the Holy Ghost], you may as well say: 'Here's my forehead, here's my beard, here's one ear and here's the other.'

Cathars sometimes attended Catholic church services to avert suspicion. The *parfait* Bélibaste reassured a Cathar believer who was uncomfortable being sprinkled with holy water: 'It can't do them [Cathars] any real harm to be sprinkled with a few drops of water. When we travel, we have to put up with much more and we don't give up on the journey.'

On the need – or otherwise – for churches, Bélibaste said: 'The heart of each person is God's true church, not the material church.' Pierre Authié remarked laughingly: 'People who bow down to idols [Catholic church statuary] are fools, because they made them themselves, these statues, with an axe and other iron tools!'

Authié told the Montaillou shepherd, Pierre Maury: 'If we preached in the churches like priests, the Roman Catholics would burn us straight away for they hate us.' When Maury asked him why the Catholics hated them so much, Authié's answer was wonderfully pragmatic and supremely confident: 'Because if we could preach publicly, the church of Rome would no longer be heard; people would prefer our faith to theirs because we speak and preach the truth while the church of Rome speaks great lies.'

Maury was convinced. He later told the inquisitor: 'They said that miracles caused by the mediation of the saints were accomplished by the Prince of this world, in other words the bad god, for whom clerics and priests built altars, churches and idols to trick people.'

It was a crime to own a copy of Cathar ritual in Occitan.

The great problem for the Catholic church was that, while the pope's organisation claimed to hold a monopoly on truth, many people preferred the stories of creation and redemption told them by the Cathars. A simple believer, questioned many years later by the Inquisition, told the story of her first contact with the *Bons Chrétiens*:

One morning Narbonne and I were sewing in front of my house and Narbonne said to me that these gentlemen [the *parfaits*] who are being hunted are Good Men and Good Christians, that they harmed nothing and nobody, not even killing animals, that they didn't lie, didn't touch women, ate neither meat nor fat and accepted persecution for the sake of God; and that they saved souls and that no one could be saved except by them.

Much of Catholic Christian belief appeared to be little more than ignorant superstition to Cathars. The Italian Cathar theologian John of Lugio later described with appalled irony the Catholic church's vision of the Last Judgment:

So there would be a multitude of children of all races, aged only four or even less, and an amazing crowd of dumb, deaf and simpletons who would never have been able to perform penitence and who would never have received from God either the ability to practise virtue or the least knowledge of Good. How and for what reason could Our Lord Jesus Christ say to them: 'Come, you have been blessed by my Father...Depart from me, you damned, to the eternal flames!'?

John of Lugio was writing around 1240, nearly a hundred years after Bernard came to preach in Albi and Toulouse. His *Liber de duobus principiis – Book of the Two Principles* – sets out clear statements of Cathar belief that could be traced back to their origins in early Bogomil teaching:

- God, who is good, cannot have created evil.
- Satan, who is evil, can do no good.
- Humankind is not guilty of original sin – sin came from Satan.
- Humans are victims of predestination and, without free will, cannot be condemned for their sins without hope of forgiveness, so there can be no everlasting Hell.
- Christ came to Earth to remind the souls trapped in Satan's 'tunics of flesh' of their true home in God's kingdom.
- The souls created by God are equal and – necessarily – good.
- With the passing of time, more and more of God's souls will escape their Earthly prison and return to God.
- The end of the world will come when all of God's souls will have made their way back to Heaven.
- There will be no Last Judgment for, at the end of the world – the end of Satan's creation – all souls will already have been saved.

What was more, the teaching of the Cathars was inclusive in another important way. Pierre Maury, the devout Cathar shepherd from Montaillou, had understood his *parfait* friend Pierre Authié's teaching very well: 'I heard it said by heretics that the souls of men and women are the same...that the only difference between them is in their bodies, which are the work of Satan.'

Bélibaste agreed: 'People received [into the Cathar church] by *Bonnes Femmes* are saved just as if they had been received by *Bons Hommes*.'

But salvation was available to all. Another Cathar priest said of the Catholic clergy: 'They were either blind or deaf, for they could neither see nor hear the voice of God for the moment. Finally, though with great pains, they would come to understand and to know their church and, in other bodies, they would recognise the truth.'

For themselves, they admitted with touching humility: 'They [the *parfaits*] said that they didn't know if they would be saved themselves, because if they converted to the faith of the church of Rome and abandoned that which was theirs today, they wouldn't be saved in their current bodies or tunics [of flesh].'

Pierre Authié characterised the two theologies by saying that the Catholic church 'withholds [salvation] and flays' while the Cathar church 'shuns [the world] and forgives'. And on the Last Judgment – whose supposed horrors were used by the Catholic church to cow its congregations – Pierre Authié said:

*A*fter the end of the world, the whole world would be full of fire, sulphur and pitch and would be consumed and he called this Hell. But all the souls of men would by then be in Paradise, and in Heaven there would be as much joy for one soul as for another; all would be one and each soul would love each other soul as much as the soul of their father, their mother or their children.

▾

⚏ CHAPTER 19 ⚏

Prayers

The Cathars had no Eucharist – no bread and wine to symbolise or become the flesh and blood of Christ. However, every time a Cathar priest broke bread, he or she recited the *Paternoster*, the Lord's Prayer, with one curious change from the prayer that most Christians know. Though the *parfait* was asking for a blessing on the meal, God had nothing to do with the food on the table, which was the work of the farmer and the baker, using the materials to hand in the corruptible material world. What the Cathar sought was the 'Word' or the 'bread of the Word', so the *parfait* would ask: 'Give us this day our supersubstantial bread.'

'Supersubstantial' means 'more than material', 'more than substantial' or 'spiritual'. 'Supersubstantial bread' isn't the 'daily bread' of survival on Earth, but knowledge of the Word, which could lead the soul back to Heaven and to God.

We know many details of the rituals of the Cathar church because three written records of their ceremonies have survived. Firstly, the work of John of Lugio – the *Liber de duobus principiis* – includes a Latin text of Cathar rituals as an appendix. Secondly, there is a Cathar Bible preserved in Lyon, written in Occitan around the beginning of the 13th century, which also includes extra pages detailing Cathar rituals. Finally, there is another collection of rites recorded in the *Dublin Cathar Ritual*, which dates from the second half of the 14th century. It was written out somewhere in the valleys of Piedmont in Italy, probably for the use of Cathar refugees fleeing the Inquisition's remorseless persecution in Languedoc. There is also a fragment of ritual in Slavon, the ancient liturgical language of the Bogomils.

Cathar priests spent a good deal of each day repeating a small number of prayers, including the *Adoremus*, the *Benedicite* – both short invocations – and the *Paternoster*, the Our Father. This was done at set hours, as in the

Catholic monasteries where the monks followed a ritual timetable of worship.

Cathar believers who had not been ordained and thereby 'freed from evil' did not have the right to pray to God on their own behalf. That was the job of their priests. When they met a Cathar, they would ask the priest three times for 'the blessing of God and your own'. With each request, they would bow or genuflect or kneel. The third time, they would add: 'Pray God for me, that He should make of me a Good Christian and lead me to a good end.'

At each request, the priests would reply: 'God's blessing upon you.' Finally, they would confirm: 'We pray God for you, that He should make of you a Good Christian and lead you to a good end.'

In Occitan, this was known as the *melhorament*, literally the 'act of improvement'. There are records of longer narrative prayers and stories, telling of the trickery of Satan, the theft of the souls from Heaven and so on. There are also examples of the *aparelhament* – Occitan for 'preparation' – which was generally carried out once a month in Cathar communities as a kind of collective confession.

The *aparelhament* and the *melhorament* were ritual exchanges, but not full sacraments. In fact, the Cathar church had only one sacrament that served its sole purpose – 'making a good end'. It was called the *consolament* or 'consolation'. They also referred to it as the 'holy baptism of Jesus Christ'. It was carried out by a Cathar priest who pronounced the words of the ritual and laid hands on the head of the supplicant. It harked back to the scene in John's Gospel, on the day of his resurrection, when Jesus appeared to his disciples and conferred on them the power to save souls:

*J*esus came and stood among them and said to them: 'Peace be with you.' When he had said this, he showed them his hands and his side. Then the disciples were glad when they saw the Lord. Jesus said to them again: 'Peace be with you. As the Father has sent me, even so I send you.' And when he had said this, he breathed on them, and said to them: 'Receive the Holy Spirit. If you forgive the sins of any, they are forgiven; if you retain the sins of any, they are retained.'

This was the task that the Cathars believed had been handed down to them in apostolic succession from Jesus's first disciples. They were to save souls through the consolation of the Holy Spirit manifest in the Word. The *consolament* included the ritual of *melhorament* as believer greeted priest. It was baptism into the Cathar church but also absolution from sin and the only possible route to the salvation of the incorruptible soul. It was used as the ceremony of entry into the Cathar priesthood for those who had served periods of fasting, contemplation, meditation and instruction as novices. For those at death's door, it was the last rites. Accompanied by vows of 'right living', it could, if they were respected, lead the soul to a 'good end'. Having received blessing, if capable, the believer would kneel and the priest would hold the New Testament on his or her head while the believer recited one *Benedicite*, three *Adoremus* and seven *Paternosters*. The priest would then read aloud from John's Gospel and lay their hands on the head of the believer as a gesture of baptism by the Holy Spirit.

The Cathars were Christians following a well-established tradition. Their success in Languedoc had turned the local Catholic church into a minority religion. So, when Lotario di Segni became Pope Innocent III in 1198, he decided to try and ensure that all Christians followed the teaching of his church and no other.

☷ CHAPTER 20 ☷

Medicine

*M*any kings and queens of the Middle Ages claimed a miraculous ability to cure illness, again through the laying on of hands. French monarchs were apparently adept at healing scrofula, a disfiguring leprous condition with ugly boils and lesions. In Britain, the king or queen's touch was supposed to cure epilepsy, while the Spanish royal family might restore the insane to their reason.

The spirit of rational scientific enquiry faded in the European Dark Ages. As a medieval Occitan proverb put it: 'The earth conceals the doctor's mistakes.'

But in other parts of the world, that was not the case, especially in the countries around the Mediterranean conquered in the extraordinary Muslim expansion that followed the death of the Prophet Mohammed. One of those countries was Egypt, home of antiquity's greatest library.

Alexandria, a city on the western side of the Nile delta, was named for Alexander the Great. When Alexander died, it became the possession of one of his generals called Ptolemy. At the beginning of the 3rd century BCE at Alexandria, Ptolemy ordered the construction of a set of buildings including a museum, a university, a military academy and a library. The work was continued by his son, Ptolemy II, who is said to have ordered copies of all the books from every land within Alexander's empire and to have employed scribes to write out by hand the contents of books carried by the ships that docked in the port and by travellers on the Egyptian roads. (The scribes gave the travellers the copy, keeping the original for the library.)

The library was repeatedly threatened or damaged by fire. There is a well-known tale of a final dreadful destruction of many of its unique texts, but historians do not agree about when this took place. Some place it as late as the 640s CE, the time of the Muslim conquest of Egypt, whether by accident or pillage.

If the library contained hieroglyphic documents, it is likely that not a single person living could read them. Among them could have been the Ebers papyrus, discovered by Western archaeologists in 1862 near the site of the city of Thebes. It dates from around 1500 BC and is a list of over 700 medicinal substances. Among the plants listed is squill – used by the Greek genius Pythagoras in the 6th century BCE as an expectorant to reduce an excess of phlegm - and liquorice, a cough remedy with soothing and anti-inflammatory properties. At the temple of Karnak at Luxor on the Nile, there are wall carvings that depict Egyptians on herb-gathering missions as far afield as Syria and Phoenicia. Of course, the doctors of ancient Egypt were often priests, too. Each stage of their treatment included rituals of cleansing or purification, for which herbs and other substances – minerals, animal dung or offal – were sometimes used.

Even if the library at Alexandria had been destroyed before the arrival of the Muslims in the city, even if the knowledge contained in hieroglyphic papyri was indecipherable, all was not lost. Many books had been translated into Greek and, in any case, much of the knowledge recorded within them was preserved in oral traditions. It is probably for this reason that, during the Crusades to the Holy Land, the medicine practised by Muslim people sometimes presented such a contrast with the efforts of the Europeans.

Usamah was a man of some authority, a Muslim knight and courtier of the administration of Saladin. Around 1175 CE, he wrote an autobiography, in which he recorded his own mild treatments and, in comparison, his appalled reaction to Crusader 'medicine':

They brought before me a knight in whose leg an abscess had grown; and a woman afflicted with imbecility. To the knight I applied a small poultice until the abscess opened and became well; and the woman I put on a diet that made her humour wet.

Then a Frankish physician came to them and said to the knight: 'Which wouldst thou prefer, living with one leg or dying with two?' The latter replied: 'Living with one leg.' The physician said: 'Bring me a strong knight and a sharp axe.'

A knight came with the axe and I was standing by. Then the physician laid the leg of the patient on a block of wood and bade the knight strike his leg with the axe and chop it off at one blow. He struck it one blow, but the leg was not severed. He dealt another blow, upon which the marrow of the leg flowed out and the patient died on the spot.

The Frankish doctor then examined the woman and said: 'This is a woman in whose head there is a devil which has possessed her. Shave off her hair.'

Accordingly they shaved it off and the woman began once more to eat their ordinary diet of garlic and mustard. Her imbecility took a turn for the worse.

The physician then said: 'The devil has penetrated through her head.' He therefore took a razor, made a deep cruciform incision on it, peeled off the skin at the middle of the incision until the bone of the skull was exposed and rubbed it with salt. The woman also expired instantly.

Thereupon I asked them whether my services were needed any longer, and when they replied in the negative I returned home, having learned of their medicine what I knew not before.

But Usamah and his brethren did not have a monopoly on effective medical treatments. He also saw successful herbal treatments used by Crusaders that he subsequently employed among his own people:

The king of the Franks had for treasurer a knight named Bernard, who (may Allah's curse be upon him!) was one of the most accursed and wicked among the Franks. A horse kicked him in the leg, which was subsequently infected and which opened in fourteen different places. Every time one of these cuts would close in one place, another would open in another place. All this happened while I was praying for his perdition.

Then came to him a Frankish physician and removed from the leg all the ointments which were on it and began to wash it with very strong vinegar. By this treatment all the cuts were healed and the man became well again. He was up again like a devil…

An artisan…had a boy whose neck was afflicted with scrofula. Every time a part of it would close, another part would open…A Frank noticed the boy and said to him: 'Wilt thou swear by thy religion that if I prescribe to you a medicine which will cure thy boy, thou wilt charge nobody fees for prescribing it thyself? In that case, I shall prescribe to you a medicine which will cure the boy.'

The man took the oath and the Frank said: 'Take uncrushed leaves of glasswort, burn them, then soak the ashes in olive oil and sharp vinegar.

Treat the scrofula with them until the spot on which it is growing is eaten up. Then take burnt lead, soak it in ghee butter and treat him with it. That will cure him.'

The father treated the boy accordingly, and the boy was cured. The sores closed and the boy returned to his normal condition of health. I have myself treated with this medicine many who were afflicted with such disease, and the treatment was successful in removing the cause of the complaint.

Glasswort is a low-growing succulent herb with tiny leaves. It tolerates immersion in salt water and is often seen carpeting estuary marshland. Also known as samphire, it is used as a vegetable with seafood and tastes a little like young spinach. The burnt glasswort leaves probably had antiseptic qualities. Vinegar is an excellent antiseptic and is still used on acne, boils and lesions.

Like today, medieval practitioners sought a panacea, a product capable of curing everything, even the incurable. In the early 12th century, that panacea was bleeding. It was applied to all kinds of illness on a series of unfortunate subjects. Often, when the victim died, it was argued that not enough blood had been taken. More than once, a battlefield surgeon gained a reputation as a good doctor simply by refraining from taking any more blood from his wounded soldiers.

As well as declining to bleed their patients to death, the better doctors used diluted vinegar to wash wounds, perhaps having discovered by accident that irrigation with wine was also a sound technique to reduce infection. Bandages that had recently been ironed – the heat killing many of the bacteria hidden in the cloth – were likewise recommended, although no one knew why this was important. In the absence of soap, doctors' assistants were encouraged to wash their hands in ash. Instead of the 'garlic and mustard' Usamah saw given in the Holy Land, effective medieval healers gave their convalescents a nutritious diet including wine made or mixed with honey, good meat cooked with spices and dried fruit and sugar-rich foods like jam and other preserves.

Meanwhile, other mainstream medieval scientists maintained that, as all things are made of a combination of basic, fundamental elements, it must be possible to transmute one into another. This 'science' of transmutation is known as alchemy and, although it figures in texts going back millennia, it seems to have become well known in the Middle Ages thanks to the publication of Arab texts.

From our modern perspective, there is a touching optimism to the futile excitement and dedication of the alchemists. But were they not simply seeking another kind of panacea – perhaps a Grail?

⛉ CHAPTER 21 ⛉

The Grail

The Grail is neither cup nor dish nor stone. It is all of these.

It first appeared in poems, to be sung or recited, called *chansons de geste* – the *geste* being a 'heroic deed'. At first, the vast majority of these epic poems dealt with the wars against the Moors and related daring and bravery from the reigns of Charles the Hammer or Charlemagne and his son Louis the Pious. The characters in the stories were limited: the righteous hero, the despicable traitor, sometimes a noble traitor, perhaps a Saracen champion or a Saracen prince, often a dusky Saracen princess. There is an 11th-century 9,000-line *chanson* called the *Song of Antioch*. In 1207, a scribe on the far side of the Pyrenees used medieval Spanish to write down the *Song of El Cid*, a noble Christian knight engaged in the *Reconquista* – the 'fight back' against the Moors in Spain.

The most famous *chanson de geste* was written about a minor skirmish that took place in the Pyrenees during Charlemagne's disastrous Spanish campaign, the *Song of Roland*. The performer would have been known as a *trouvère* – the 'author of the work' – or perhaps a *jongleur* – literally a 'juggler', a humble performer rather than an author.

The *chansons de geste* were seen as important historical authorities to many of the people who listened to them and they often included tales of the foundation of states and dynasties. Around a hundred of them have survived to this day, many of them in multiple copies, laboriously written out in manuscript by scribes, some illuminated with as much care as a spiritual document.

It was in an epic poem of the 12th century that the first reference to the Grail legend appeared – *Li conte del Graal*. The poem was by Chrétien of Troyes, a French poet and *trouvère*. The story is perhaps best known because it focuses on a knight of the court of King Arthur called Perceval. It was also

A 15th-century vision of
Chrétien's Perceval.

the first mention of the love affair between Queen Guinevere and Lancelot.

Chrétien was a servant of the countess of Champagne, the daughter of Eleanor of Aquitaine. (Troyes was the capital of Champagne, east of Paris, one of the most important Cathar regions outside of Languedoc.) *Li conte del Graal* was Chrétien's fifth major work and he began it around 1180. Some people believe that Chrétien's work contains Kabbalistic symbols and that he was originally Jewish but converted to Christianity.

The poem in Chrétien's hand is incomplete. He worked on it until about 1183, when it contained roughly 9,000 lines. He dedicated the unfinished work to his patron, Philip, the count of Flanders, who had recently returned from a Crusade to the Holy Land. In his opening verses, he thanks Philip for showing him a mysterious book that served as the inspiration for his Grail story. No one knows if this document ever really existed but the story proved extremely intriguing. Several other poets immediately embarked on continuations of Chrétien's poem, adding more than 50,000 lines up until about 1191. One of these poets claimed that Chrétien had stopped writing because he was dead. In 1190, Philip of Flanders returned to Palestine to die at the siege of Acre. There would be no more mysterious revelations from Chrétien's patron.

Li conte del Graal is the story of Perceval, a young and pure Welsh knight of the Round Table. After a series of adventures in which he saves a maiden and gains in wisdom and self-knowledge, he meets the Fisher King, who takes him to his castle and offers him dinner. Before the meal is served, Perceval is asked to sit quietly and observe a strange procession: a young man with a blooded lance; two boys carrying candelabra; a beautiful young woman carrying an ornately decorated silver *graal* – in old French a 'cup' or 'flattish dish' – which contains a miraculous wafer capable of healing the Fisher King's wounded father. Perceval asks no questions, sleeps through the night, wakes alone and returns to Camelot. Back at King Arthur's court, Perceval is soon taken to task by a revolting old crone – a stock medieval character known as a 'loathly lady' – for not having questioned the Fisher King more closely. She says this would have led to the injured king being healed. The loathly lady also tells him of other quests undertaken by King Arthur's knights. The story continues with the tale of Gawain, Arthur's nephew, whose more pragmatic decisions contrast with Perceval's innocence. Finally, Chrétien returns to the tale of Perceval, who meets with a hermit – his own uncle – who teaches him spiritual enlightenment and some of the mysteries of the Grail.

That is the end of the story told by Chrétien. The continuations cover Gawain and then, later, Perceval visiting the *château du Graal*. Perceval repairs the legendary sword Trebuchet but it retains a tiny flaw – just as Perceval's soul is yet flawed. Lancelot's romance with Guinevere and his quest for the Grail is told. The Fisher King dies and Perceval ascends his throne for just seven years. Finally, Perceval departs into the forest to die, taking with him the ornately decorated *graal* and the blooded lance.

Another evolution of the Grail story came from Robert of Boron. Robert's version of the story became so popular that it was soon the standard history of King Arthur's court. He began it around 1190 and wove Chrétien's mystical *graal* into a Christian Arthurian romance where the low silver dish of the original is transformed imaginatively into the cup used by Christ at the Last Supper – the Holy Chalice.

Robert says the Holy Chalice was used by Joseph of Arimathea to collect drops of blood from the wounded side of Christ as he hung on the cross, pierced in the side by the Roman centurion's lance. Joseph of Arimathea then brought the cup, now known as the Holy Grail, to Avalon – Glastonbury – where it was hidden away in expectation of the coming of King Arthur and the Grail knight Perceval. Other, much later, authors have suggested that Joseph brought it to southern France, perhaps accompanied by Mary Magdalene – even by Christ himself. They are said to have visited Chartres, too.

There is also, in Languedoc, a legend of the Holy Grail that tells that it was made of wood by Adam, the first man. This simple cup was Adam's sole legacy to his son and was passed down through the generations, ultimately to Jesus. It was this wooden cup that Christ used at the Last Supper and it was, therefore, this wooden cup that, after Christ's crucifixion, is said to have travelled with Mary Magdalene and Joseph of Arimathea to the south of France.

But Christian tradition leaves out Joseph altogether. For Christians, the Holy Chalice only contained the wine of the Last Supper, a symbol of Christ's blood, not actually his blood. The cup was then taken away by the apostle Peter, who used it in early Christian services in the Holy Land and Antioch, then carried it on to Rome, where he continued evangelising.

The persuasiveness of Peter's teaching must have been reinforced by the fact that he could hold in his hand a cup used by Christ on Earth, one of a dwindling number of people still alive to have known Jesus. He died around 64 CE, some thirty years after Christ, the year of the great fire of Rome, when the Emperor Nero is supposed to have taken no action to control the flames, preferring to 'fiddle'. Some believe that Nero started the fire. Certainly he used it as a stick with which to beat the Christians and Peter was thought of as the Christian 'bishop of Rome'. Executed by crucifixion – at his own request upside down in order not to mimic the death of Christ – Peter is said to have passed on the throne of bishop and, with it, the sainted relics of the life of Jesus, including the Holy Chalice.

In the Christian story, the chalice was handed on from bishop of Rome to bishop of Rome in an unbroken line of apostolic succession until 258 CE, when the Roman emperor Valerian demanded that the Christians hand over all their relics. The Holy Chalice was then sent into safety, probably in Spain. There is even a complex sequence of events that brings the Holy Chalice into the hands of Charlemagne on his Spanish campaign against the Moors towards the end of the 8th century.

Also writing at the end of the 12th century, in the decade after Chrétien's death, Wolfram von Eschenbach expressed contempt for Chrétien's work and claims his own separate source. In his writings, Wolfram claims – paradoxically – to have been illiterate and says that he dictated his work to a scribe. Few believe this.

Wolfram's poem – *Parzival* – is the story of Perceval and Gawain and is clearly derived, at least in part, from *Li conte del Graal*. In fact, Wolfram takes enormous trouble to define precisely what the Grail is and how it functions, developing Chrétien's scene between Perceval and his uncle.

Perceval meets a holy man, a hermit named Trevrizent. He learns that he cannot demand God's assistance and must accept his trials and humbly pray for aid, without expectation. Trevrizent tells Perceval that the Grail is a stone of incalculable value imbued with youth and strength, renewed each year on Good Friday, the day of Christ's death, by a wafer of communion bread from Heaven. Sometimes instructions for the Grail knights will appear on the stone and none can use the power of the Grail: only the Grail can call knights into its service to become the Grail king. Any called by the Grail will be of a special bloodline.

It is in Wolfram's work that we discover a Grail guarded by Knights Templar, an organisation of huge renown at the end of the 12th century but which had only been founded three or four generations earlier. *Parzival* also introduces the Munsalwäsche, a great castle that is, at one and the same time, the house of God and the house of the Grail. Finally, *Parzival* was the inspiration for the libretto of Richard Wagner's last opera, *Parsifal*, in which he famously renamed the Grail castle Monsalvat, creating – so it is said – a veiled reference to the Cathars' final refuge at Montségur. (Wagner had already used Wolfram as a character in an earlier opera – *Tannhäuser*.)

Like Robert of Boron and Chrétien of Troyes, Wolfram von Eschenbach's work was fantastically popular. There are more than eighty surviving manuscript copies of the thirteen books of Wolfram's *Parzival* alone. But the stories are, basically, in competition with one another. Each – and there are others that refer to the Grail – has its own 'spin' on the mystical object. Each author – especially Chrétien – clothes the Grail legend in a perhaps symbolic tale of quest, combat, guilt and self-knowledge. The goal of the quest is not simply an object or marriage with a 'pure maiden'. Had Perceval closely questioned his host about the strange procession of candles, lance and *graal*, he could have healed the sickness in the kingdom. Whatever form the Grail takes – dish, cup or stone, or perhaps some other shape – possession of it gives life to those who have achieved enlightenment.

The path to enlightenment is through knowledge. Within a generation of the death of Chrétien and while Robert of Boron and Wolfram von Eschenbach were still writing, two poets of the *langue d'oc* – one a famous name, the other clouded in mystery – were singing contrasting songs of the Crusade against the Cathars – *La Canso de la Crosada*. This extraordinary document has ensured, for 800 years, that history, in this case, would not only be written by the victors.

CHAPTER 22

Abundance and Fasts

arcassonne is the capital of the *département* of the Aude, named after the river that slices the modern city of Carcassonne in two. Because of its location between two mountain ranges, the Aude is windy. Carcassonne has more than twenty days of storms each year, for the same reason. All the same, thunder and lightning are generally accompanied by heavy vertical rain, as the storms often arrive when the wind drops. Morning fog and low cloud sometimes prevent planes from landing at the city's airport.

The Carcassonne hill is in the centre of a fertile plain. But to the south of the Cité, following the Aude upstream into the Corbières and the Pyrenees, the landscape soon changes. The river becomes a torrent, the road perched precariously alongside as it winds up through natural gorges. In these hills and mountains snow is common.

At the turn of the millennium – remarkably – the weather was completely different. Between the 10th and 14th centuries BCE, Europe enjoyed what scientists call the medieval warm period, or Little Climatic Optimum. Its effects were not felt worldwide – the climate in equatorial East Africa was dry and temperatures in Antarctica lower than the long-term average – but the Vikings sailed across seas free of ice and colonised Greenland and other northern lands. Red grapes were grown in Europe as far north as southern Britain.

In Languedoc, cultivation of all kinds of crops edged, season by season, year by year, up the mountainsides. Peasants and artisans colonised land above 1,800 metres perhaps for the first time, establishing some of the extraordinary villages of the High Pyrenees. How inhospitable they seem today – but not then. Snow-bound passes became practicable, especially for shepherds and goatherds, who could honestly be said to have no nationality at all, wintering on the sunward side of the mountains in Aragon and summering to the north.

All the same, the diet of even the best-fed medieval peasant was very different from that available in the same countryside today. In 12th-century Europe there was no corn or maize, no kidney or haricot beans, no tomatoes or potatoes, no sunflowers, no courgettes, no cocoa, no sweet or hot peppers. All these products were only introduced after the 1492 voyage of Christopher Columbus to the New World. Shallots, apricots, oranges, some spices and candied sugar were all by-products of the ongoing Crusades to the Near East. Sugar was an expensive luxury, mostly used as a medicinal ingredient and was replaced in food preparation by honey.

At the time of the Crusade against the Cathars, the staples were lentils, broad beans, chickpeas, various grains, oil, olives, salt, carrots, leeks, garlic and onions. They enjoyed fruit and nuts in season, especially apples, pears, grapes and medlars − an unusual native fruit that must be ripened off the tree to acquire a honey-like flavour − walnuts, hazelnuts and sweet chestnuts. They also ate the flowerbuds of cardoons, a thistle related to the globe artichoke, whose hearts were sometimes blanched by being wrapped or buried in the ground. In springtime, when the winter stocks were nearly exhausted, early root vegetables − perhaps turnips or radishes − were eaten. The seeds of these tubers provided rapeseed oil, which was used in 13th-century lamps. They ate *blé* − 'grains' − including wheat, barley, rye or *méteil*, a mixed crop of wheat and rye. Despite the Little Optimum, *la viande* − 'meat' − was a luxury reserved mainly for the great houses who hunted or as a periodic treat. Fresh and salt-water fish were available.

Food that needed cooking in water was boiled in pans made of *terre grise* − a kind of grey terracotta. The lids of the better-quality pots made such a good seal that they were virtually pressure cookers. Iron pans were used for frying or for cooking dry flat breads, which were also baked in ovens of clay brick. Throughout Languedoc, wood was always available, but it had to be cut and seasoned for a really good fire. Charcoal burners burnt firewood in dense heaps, which deprived the flames of oxygen, giving an efficient, lightweight fuel.

Visiting Languedoc today, many *restaurateurs* offer *cassoulet* − a stew made with white haricot beans and duck, goose, pork, bacon and sausage and a sauce based on tomatoes. If there was a medieval version, it must have been cooked with dried broad beans. Some say it was first brought to France in the 12th century by Arabs, who added the beans to lamb stew to make it stretch further. The inhabitants of Castelnaudary claim it was first cooked during the Hundred Years War when the city was besieged. The dish was apparently the result of cooking everything they had left in a single big *casserole* – a terracotta cooking pot – whence the name. In Toulouse and Carcassonne, whose inhabitants also claim to have invented the dish, there is agreement that if you stick a wooden spoon in a 'proper' *cassoulet*, it will stand up on its own.

Despite the abundance, many religious groups chose to limit their what they ate. The Cathars of Languedoc – like the Catholics who lived alongside them – enjoyed a diet made up of whatever was in season or could be preserved by salt, smoke, drying or pickling. If they were preparing to 'make a good end' – in other words, preparing for death – they might alter their diet as a consequence. Some historians – including contemporaries of the Crusade against the Cathars – have misunderstood this fasting *in extremis* and claimed that it was a form of suicide or, at the very least, a way of hastening death. In fact, there is at least one record of the fast having the opposite effect. The lucky believer saved from death's door immediately went and tucked into a substantial meal.

Some religious orders insisted that their flocks should follow their lead – not the Cathars. This difference between what was expected of the priests and what was expected of the flock was one of the many ways in which the Cathar church managed to be, at one and the same time, tolerant and ascetic, self-righteous and indulgent. The Cathar priests themselves, ordained using virtually the same ceremony of *consolament* that served as their last rites, led lives of poverty, chastity and manual labour, and were restricted to an ascetic vegetarian diet and regular fasts to accompany their cycles of prayer and devotion. But they expected their communities to live ordinary, perhaps irreligious lives. They rejoiced, however, when one of their number found the courage, faith and determination to take the great step into the priesthood.

In their privations, the Cathars weren't so very different from the most committed Catholics. But the Cathars' diet was determined by a Creation story that, tellingly, had nothing to do with a mythical Garden of Eden, a talking snake, a tree of knowledge or a magic apple.

The Cathars believed in a Creation made entirely of spirit, made entirely by God, who is also entirely spirit. The spirit Creation is entirely good and no evil can come from it. The same was true of God – entirely good, entirely spirit. Therefore God was not of or in this world of pain, suffering and death, neither as Himself, or in the sun or rain, the plentiful harvest or the stillborn child, or in the churches, the crosses or the shrines. The 14th-century

Cathar Pierre Authié put it in terms the local Pyrenean farmers could easily understand: 'It isn't God who brought forth this fine wheat crop; He has nothing to do with it! What brings forth a good wheat crop is the manure you dig into the soil.'

So what happened to the souls of the dead – the incorruptible, indestructible souls? The answer is that they passed, after an interval of about four days, into another creature, perhaps not a human being – so Cathars would not eat the meat, eggs or milk of any animal. They would eat fish, however, which they believed incapable of receiving a transmigrating soul. In common with most of medieval Europe, they were unaware that fish bred through sexual reproduction; they thought they grew in the water like plants.

The Catholic Cistercians repudiated meat and ate fish but if a brother fell ill, he would be allowed to take animal products, even on feast days. The Cathars' rule, however, was absolute. Habitually, on every second day, the Cathar priests semi-fasted by eating only bread and water. Three times each year they undertook a Lenten fast, rather than just once from Ash Wednesday to Good Friday.

The drawn, ascetic appearance of the itinerant Cathar priests is a constant refrain in the accounts we have of their lives. That said, there are also many accounts of Cathar priests feasting in the houses of their faithful – at least in the periods between the great persecutions. Of course, they would only eat the foods they were allowed, so the greatest favourites were fish dishes – eel and trout caught fresh in the mountain rivers or, from the coast, dried or salted conger eel, hake, cod, skate and sea bass. They ate them in pâtés or baked in a pastry case – *en croûte*.

Wine was permitted at any time and was drunk, generally, with water. It would accompany feasts served in great halls or the meanest meals of bread and cabbage. It was carried on the medieval peasants' incessant trudges from village to town and from river to field, the settlements each a day's march apart. It was used to soak stale crusts, which must not be wasted but which, otherwise, couldn't be swallowed. If an injured animal or a lucky shot with a sling did bring meat to the table – and if, by chance, no Cathar priests were in the neighbourhood – the faithful would enjoy the unaccustomed treat without guilt, even in the midst of Lent. When the table was meagre, the faithful could at least enjoy a sense of superiority, looking down on the 'savage' Catholics and their 'bestial' addiction to flesh.

Every meal began with a ritual blessing and sharing of bread, in memory of the Last Supper, and a recitation of the Lord's Prayer. The Cathar Pierre of Gaillac told his – I expect – somewhat baffled inquisitor: 'They said that the bread placed on the altar and blessed with the words of Christ at the Last Supper with His apostles was not the true body of Christ…The bread of which Christ spoke…was the Word of God.'

More than once in his poignant and contradictory career as a guerrilla priest, the last Cathar, Guilhem Bélibaste, aroused suspicion by refusing food he wasn't allowed to eat. He thought the communion bread was just as futile as his colleagues, but on days of fast he did not deny its secondary attractions: 'I wonder how it can help to save a sick person's soul. After all, this piece of bread, still in their stomach, will be buried with their body and rot just the same. On the other hand, I'd eat plenty, if offered!'

CHAPTER 23

Raymond-Roger Trencavel

The political and – to a certain extent – religious independence of Languedoc can be summed up in a single word – Trencavel.

Bernard-Aton Trencavel IV died in 1129 CE, succeeded by Roger I. The Château Comtal – the castle on the western side of the Cité on the Hill – was begun in 1130 on foundations and Gallo-Roman towers established in the first centuries after Christ.

The walls of Carcassonne were thick and tall, at the top of the rise of land the Cité had occupied for millennia. Narrow gateways, or posterns, guarded access, easily closed and reinforced. The main entrance to the city – the Porte Narbonnaise – was surmounted by the Trencavel seal. (Today, the ensign of the house has been replaced by a statue of the Virgin Mary.) Here and there, the walls were extended into barbicans, semicircular projections each with their own guards and postern.

In the middle of the 12th century, around the time of the disastrous Second Crusade to the Holy Land, the family territory was fragmented as parts of the domains were handed over to Roger I's brother, Bernard-Aton V, viscount of Nîmes and Agde. Roger I was viscount of only Albi, Béziers, Carcassonne and Razès, and was shortly succeeded by another brother, Raymond I. Raymond I married Adélaïde and one of their children, Cécile, married into the house of Foix, the impregnable Pyrenean stronghold. This tightly woven tapestry of family bonds would become a crucial element in the defence of Languedoc against the Catholic church and the French king.

After the death of Adélaïde, Raymond remarried and had a son, the future Roger II. Roger II married another Adélaïde, also known as Azalaïs, the daughter of Raymond V of Toulouse. (Perhaps Adélaïde and Trencavel met at the Council of Lombers in 1176, invited by the Catholic bishop of

Albi to debate the merits of Catholic and Cathar doctrines.) To bind the families of Toulouse and Trencavel one notch tighter together, Raymond Trencavel I's younger sister, Béatrix, later married Raymond VI of Toulouse, the brother of Adélaïde.

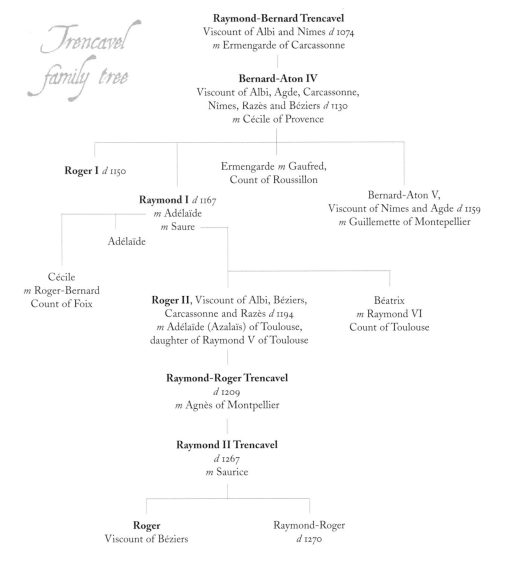

Raymond-Bernard Trencavel
Viscount of Albi and Nîmes *d* 1074
m Ermengarde of Carcassonne

Bernard-Aton IV
Viscount of Albi, Agde, Carcassonne,
Nîmes, Razès and Béziers *d* 1130
m Cécile of Provence

Roger I *d* 1150

Ermengarde *m* Gaufred,
Count of Roussillon

Bernard-Aton V,
Viscount of Nîmes and Agde *d* 1159
m Guillemette of Montepellier

Raymond I *d* 1167
m Adélaïde
m Saure

Adélaïde

Cécile
m Roger-Bernard
Count of Foix

Roger II, Viscount of Albi, Béziers,
Carcassonne and Razès *d* 1194
m Adélaïde (Azalaïs) of Toulouse,
daughter of Raymond V of Toulouse

Béatrix
m Raymond VI
Count of Toulouse

Raymond-Roger Trencavel
d 1209
m Agnès of Montpellier

Raymond II Trencavel
d 1267
m Saurice

Roger
Viscount of Béziers

Raymond-Roger
d 1270

Bernard of Clairvaux was made a saint in 1174, coincidentally the year of the birth of Pedro II of Aragon, Spanish feudal lord of the house of Trencavel in its lands of Carcassonne and Razès. In 1185, Roger II, viscount of Albi, Béziers, Carcassonne and Razès, and his wife, Adélaïde, daughter of

Raymond V of Toulouse, had a son, Raymond-Roger Trencavel. When Roger II died, Raymond-Roger was given a guardian and tutor, a Cathar believer called Bertrand from Saisssac in the Montagne Noire. As far as we know, Raymond-Roger was never 'consoled', but he grew up in a tradition of tolerance and chivalry.

Raymond-Roger Trencavel lived a prosperous and fulfilled existence. He married – as was a habit in his family – a woman of the south, Agnès of Montpellier. They had a son, born in 1204 or thereabouts, known as Raymond II. At two years old, Raymond-Roger of Foix became the little boy's tutor. (The *comté* of Foix, though theoretically vassal of Pedro II of Aragon, looked down on the squabbles and treaties of the lowlands from its impregnable Pyrenean fortress.)

Raymond-Roger Trencavel had the allegiance of many of the minor lords round about – Cabaret, Bram, Minerve, Termes, Lavaur and others. Each called Trencavel 'lord'. Each knew his place in the feudal scheme just as Raymond-Roger knew his. Though inherited by Raymond-Roger, the domains of Albi and Béziers were part of the county of Toulouse. Therefore Trencavel owed allegiance to Raymond of Toulouse and Raymond, in his turn, owed the protection of a feudal lord to Trencavel. At the same time, the lands of Carcassonne and Razès were allowed to Trencavel by the house of Aragon and its king, Pedro II.

In feudal relations, the ability to convert theoretical power into real clout through the use of military force was vital. When the Crusaders came, Trencavel at first believed that he would be protected by Toulouse and Aragon. He was wrong. But despite the frailty of the consciences of his lords, Raymond-Roger Trencavel felt a great responsibility to his subjects. In fact, that sense of duty seems to have extended beyond the normal limits of feudal lordship.

Up until 2004, the seal of Raymond-Roger Trencavel had been a well-known historical artefact. Its form was recognised by scholars and tourists. This was, however, a mistake. The seal that everyone took to be that of the defender of Carcassonne was in fact that of his defeatist brother, Raymond-Roger II, the man who, once the Cité was lost, signed away the family's viscounty.

The discovery came about, as sometimes they do, by chance. A scholar by the name of Laurent Macé was conducting research into one of his areas of interest – medieval seals – in the archive of the Knights Hospitaller of Jerusalem in Toulouse. In the Hospitaller archive, Macé discovered two official documents, dated 1185 and 1202, imprinted with the seal of Raymond-Roger Trencavel. The image is of a galloping *chevalier* – including his steed – who brandishes a long sword with a round pommel in his right hand. It is, at one and the same time, a symbol of feudal authority and warlike intent. In this, it fits the image of Trencavel handed down to us by his willingness to protect the weak and stand up to the Crusaders against dreadful odds. He did this alone, even after the defection of his liege lords, Raymond of Toulouse and Pedro of Aragon.

Then, when he knew all was lost, he sacrificed himself for his people.

▣ CHAPTER 24 ▣
The Humiliation of Raymond VI

he Crusades to Jerusalem didn't fight heretics, they fought infidels. The Saracens slaughtered by the First Crusade in the Holy City were 'wrong'. They were not, however, as 'wrong' as the Cathars, because, for the Catholic church, the Cathars knew God's Word and chose not to accept it.

The word 'heresy' comes from the Greek, meaning 'choice'. The Cathars chose to teach, for example, that it was ridiculous for babies, without any sense of right or wrong, to be baptised into the church and for someone else to affirm their faith for them. They taught that God was wholly good, that nothing bad – illness, misfortune, drought, flood – could come from Him. They taught that there is nothing of God in our bodies, but that our souls are wholly His, and that every soul, without exception, would – eventually – be saved and return to God. Their priests lived in poverty and chastity supported by their own labour while, they claimed, the Catholics 'racketeer and take the people's tithes and their first fruits, without having done a stroke of their own work'.

His Holiness Pope Innocent III claimed to be the head of the 'one Universal Church of the faithful, outside of which there is absolutely no salvation'.

The faithful of the Cathar flock believed: 'These preachers they are hunting down are *Bons Chrétiens* who do no harm to anybody. They will not kill any kind of animal or lie or eat meat or fat and they endure persecution for God's sake; and they save souls – none can be saved without their blessing.'

What gave Innocent the right? How did this man reconcile the teaching of Jesus with the violence he preached? Did he imagine the victims, the people of southwest France, with their prosperous agricultural economy,

Innocent III excommunicates the Albigenses, as shown in the Chroniques de France ou de Saint Denis, *which dates from the second quarter of the 14th century.*

bustling towns, religious tolerance, the itinerant *trobadors* with their songs and poems of noble combat and courtly love, the emerging chivalric code? Did he know that, in the lands we call Languedoc, women could own and trade property and retained ownership of their dowries and could spend or invest independently of their husbands' will?

Innocent was not ignorant of the culture of Languedoc. For some time he had been putting pressure on Raymond VI of Toulouse to act against the Cathars. On several occasions, Raymond promised to act, but never did. On 10 March 1204, Innocent wrote to the king of France: 'It is your responsibility to harry the count of Toulouse out of those lands which at present he occupies; and to place them in the hands of true Catholics who will be enabled, under your beneficent rule, to serve our Lord in all faithfulness.'

Innocent knew that the Catholic church was failing to convert the people, that his priests made a poor impression on potential believers and that his monasteries appeared acquisitive and slothful. He knew, too, that the noble houses of Languedoc were tolerant of Catharism or actual converts to the 'heretic' religion and that it had spread through the complex web of interlinked family trees throughout the plains and up into the hills and mountains. So he sent a personal emissary – a legate – with a double objective: to revitalise the Catholic clergy of the region and to browbeat Raymond VI of Toulouse into acting to suppress the church of the *Bons Chrétiens*. The legate's name was Peter of Castelnau.

Peter was a Cistercian monk from the abbey of Fontfroide, between Carcassonne and Narbonne. He made few friends. He was at once unworldly – his diplomatic skills were non-existent – but at the same time completely sure of himself. He infuriated the local Roman Catholic bishops – his natural allies – by telling them that it was their inactivity and lack of apostolic zeal that had made room for the success of the Cathar church. In 1205, he suspended from office the bishops of Béziers and Viviers, then ordered proceedings against Bérenger II, archbishop of Narbonne. At the same time, Raymond of Toulouse complained bitterly of the humiliation of being harangued by the pedantic, self-righteous monk.

Raymond VI ruled his lands independently of the northern French monarchy, of whom he was rightly suspicious. He was a sworn vassal of his kinsman Pedro II of Aragon, ruler of a kingdom that straddled the Pyrenees. His sister Adélaïde was the mother of Raymond-Roger Trencavel, lord of Carcassonne, his nephew and his vassal. Trencavel was also a vassal of Aragon. Within Raymond's lands and – especially – those of Trencavel and the Pyrenean enclave of Foix, there was a tradition of political independence that led to a climate of religious tolerance.

The Cathar 'heresy' thrived alongside business, industry and every sort of art and craft. In the larger cities – Toulouse, Narbonne, Avignon, Montpellier, Béziers – there were schools of medicine, mathematics, philosophy and astrology. They were home to large, successful Jewish communities too. Records show a Doctor Abraham from Beaucaire giving lectures, as well as a respected scholar named Simeon and a Rabbi Jacob. Also at Toulouse, the course on Aristotle embodied recent discoveries by Arab philosophers.

Raymond VI of Toulouse is known to historians as 'more diplomat than warrior'. He continued to prevaricate, enraging the papal legate, Peter of Castelnau. Finally, despite his heavy-handedness, towards the end of 1207 Peter managed to establish a league of southern barons who agreed to hunt down the 'heretics'. Progress was limited and, as the months went by, Peter demanded with increasing shrillness that Raymond should join in the brutal persecution of his own subjects. He refused and, in January 1208, at a stormy interview at the church of Saint-Gilles in Raymond's lands in the Rhône valley, Castelnau publicly excommunicated him.

This was no mere symbolic, spiritual punishment. The pope had given Peter the right to act in the name of the Catholic church. Excommunication would lead directly to a more basely material sentence: 'As to the property of the condemned...let it be confiscated.'

The meeting broke up and the two delegations retired to their respective camps. We do not know what deliberations took place there. The following morning, in a chill mist that rose from the mighty river, just as the papal party was about to cross the Rhône, an officer in the service of the count of Toulouse ran Peter of Castelnau through. He died on the spot. No one knows for certain if the officer was acting on Raymond's orders or at his own initiative. Whatever the case, it brought disaster on the houses of Toulouse, Trencavel and Aragon – and on the Cathars.

The murder of Peter of Castelnau gave Innocent the excuse he needed to preach the Crusade. In return for forty days' continuous service alongside the Mediterranean, the 'soldier of Christ' would be granted absolution for a lifetime of sin. Whilst on the Crusade, the property the Crusaders left behind – in France, Flanders, Bavaria, England or elsewhere – would remain under the protection of the Catholic church. Crusades to the Holy Land were dangerous and survival doubtful. The alternative of forty days' service close to home proved popular. The fertile lands and industrious people of the south were ripe for conquest.

Raymond the diplomat tried to halt the Crusade by submitting publicly to Innocent's will. He agreed to perform an Act of Submission at the symbolic location of Saint-Gilles, where Peter had been murdered and buried. (A year after the murder, Peter's brother Cistercians had exhumed his corpse and found it intact and imbued with an 'odour of sanctity'. Some say his body was then taken to be reburied at Fontfroide.)

The ceremony took place in June 1209 in the presence of three archbishops, nineteen bishops and numerous other dignitaries. Between the two great lions that guard entry to the west door of the church were set out various relics of Christ and his saints. Raymond of Toulouse, wearing a penitent's garb – a cord round his neck, a candle in his hand and stripped to the waist – was brought into the square. He swore – on the relics – allegiance to the pope and his legates. The pope's representative then draped his stole round Raymond's neck, gave him absolution and marched him into the church, beating him around the shoulders with a bundle of birch twigs.

To persuade the pope to lift the excommunication, Raymond agreed to a list of humiliating clauses that transferred many of his rights as count to the legates. He was required to offer apologies to every bishop and abbot with whom he was in conflict and relinquish his rights over bishoprics and religious houses throughout his domain. He had to disband the militia of veterans and mercenaries he employed to protect his territories and no longer entrust any Jew with public office. He was obliged to cease protecting 'heretics' and deliver them up to the Crusaders and to regard as heretics all those denounced by ecclesiastical authority.

The list continued but, even if he had wanted to, Raymond couldn't fulfil the intransigent demands. There were towns within his lands in which the Cathar 'heretics' probably made up a majority of his subjects. What was more, the persecution was also patently unjust. When Foulques, the Catholic bishop of Toulouse, asked the *chevalier* Pons Adhemar why the nobles of Languedoc did not break up the nests of 'heretics' in their territories, Adhemar replied: 'We cannot do it. We were all brought up together. Many of them are related to us. Besides, we can see for ourselves that they live decent, honourable lives.'

In June 1209, inside the church of Saint-Gilles, Raymond was obliged to promise to pitch his tent in the camp of the *Ost gran* – the great Host – of Crusaders. The crowd outside the building became so densely packed that, when the time came to leave, Raymond and the legate had to sneak out through the crypt, passing the spot where Peter of Castelnau had briefly been buried.

Raymond would not take part in the massacre at Béziers the following month or at the siege of impregnable Carcassonne in August but he had, all the same, betrayed his people. It would not be long before he regretted his decision and changed camp again. But, by then, for the Cathars of Languedoc, it was probably too late. Too many powers had learnt to covet their souls and their lands. When Raymond finally died, he was forbidden burial in hallowed ground. His coffin stood out of doors for years until it was destroyed by rats and his bones were lost.

CHAPTER 25

The Massacre at Béziers

Rome, for the longest time people have said that
Your head has been shrinking every time you shave your tonsure.
For me, I think it would do you a lot of good,
Rome, if they cut out your brain,
Because you wear a really mean hat,
You and Cîteaux, since in Béziers you ordered
That appalling butchery.

This is part of a poem written by a young Occitan *trobador* called
Guilhem Figueiras who was alive at the time of the 'appalling
butchery'. It was common currency in Languedoc and, more than
sixty years later, a 'heretic' Toulouse merchant was prosecuted for, among
other things, possession of a copy of the New Testament in Latin and
French and a manuscript of Guilhem Figueiras' song against Rome.

The city of Béziers was built on a hill, at its highest point about 60 metres
above the flood plain of the river Hérault, but alongside one of its
tributaries, the Orb. The Mediterranean Sea is just 20 kilometres to the
south, the southern tip of the Massif Central about 50 kilometres to the
north. Although not quite as old as Carcassonne, the hill was also first
occupied by Stone Age hunter-gatherers. During the Iron Age and up to the
2nd century BC, it developed as a Celtic population centre and the first walls
were built on the slopes. In the next century, it became an important Roman
city in the province of Gallia Narbonensis – a region roughly equivalent to
what we now know as Languedoc. When the Romans built the Via
Domitia, Béziers became a staging post on the route from Italy to Spain
along the Mediterranean Sea.

At the fall of the Western Roman Empire, like Carcassonne, Béziers passed into the hands of the Visigoths, then was taken by Muslims around the beginning of the 8th century. The Muslim advance climbed all the way north up through France to the Loire valley, where Charlemagne's grandfather, Charles the Hammer, defeated them at Tours. Then he swept south, driving the Muslim forces back towards Spain. In the conflict for Béziers, the city was ruined.

But the place was rebuilt and Charlemagne decided the city merited its own county. Time passed and Béziers grew. By the 12th century it was an important prize in the ongoing feudal conflict between Toulouse and Aragon. The Trencavel family attempted to negotiate a safe course between the two great houses. But neither Raymond-Roger Trencavel's grandfather nor his father had to face the scale of threat that, in 1209, was bearing down on Raymond-Roger.

The verse chronicler Guilhèm of Tudèla described how the *Ost gran* – the great Host – assembled in Lyon in the spring of 1209:

*T*he abbot of Cîteaux was among the horsemen with his archbishops and many lettered persons. The duke of Burgundy and his pairs and army spread their banners. The count of Nevers raised his standards, the count of Saint-Paul had his armed men and the count of Auxerre all his followers, Guillaume of Geneva, blessed by his lands, Adhémar of Poitiers…came with all his people and Pierre Bermons d'Anduze. It would take me more than a day to tell all their names, those of Provence, from distant lands, from close at hand who came to take the cross. There were so many, they were impossible to count.

The organised army and the mob of hangers-on snaked down the valley of the Rhône, then along the Via Domitia west towards Montpellier. There they paused and Raymond VI of Toulouse abandoned his kinsman Raymond-Roger Trencavel and joined the camp of the Crusaders. Each knight wore a cross of red cloth on his chest. Guilhèm estimated the strength of the Host:

La òst fo meravilhosa e grans, si m'ajut fes:
Vint melia cavaliers, armatz de totas res,
E plus de docent melia, que vilas que pages;
En cels no comti ni clergies ni borzes.

The host was wondrously large, trust me:
20,000 knights, armed to the teeth,
And more than 200,000 from cities and countryside;
And that without counting either clergy or bourgeois.

It was a monstrous company, a vast 'serpent of weapons'. Raymond-Roger decided to go to Béziers and put the city in defensive order. At the same time, he would try to arrange a meeting with Raymond VI of Toulouse.

The Host surged into abominable movement once more. Raymond-Roger was obliged to abandon Béziers. He asked the people of the city – the Biterrois – to fight with energy and courage – '*a fòrça e a vertu*'. Palisades were built and ditches dug. One of the canons of the Catholic cathedral asked Trencavel: 'Who will defend you from the forces of Heaven?' He replied that the city was impregnable, that the inhabitants could live for a month on their stores and the Host would be obliged to move on in search of rations. His bailiff and private secretary, the Jew Samuel, agreed. Raymond-Roger promised the Biterrois that he would return from Carcassonne with an army of reinforcements 'just as soon as I have assembled my vassals'.

The people of Béziers had confidence in Trencavel. They were convinced that their city, perched on a steep hill with imposing walls and plentiful stores, could withstand a siege. The determination of the inhabitants to resist was firm. Trencavel's bailiff, Samuel, told his master he should take with him to Carcassonne all those who wished to leave. A few Jews followed with one or two Cathars. Refugees from Narbonne, the city next in line to be threatened, joined them.

The Catholic bishop of Béziers attempted to encourage the people to prepare to hand over the 'heretics' to the Host, but they refused: 'You are nothing but wolves disguised as lambs!'

The words of the *Bons Chrétiens* must have been fresh in their minds:

The true Christians are those who do not kill, not even an animal, who don't lie, who don't swear oaths, who respect the precepts of the Gospels. We are the true apostles of Christ. In this world, of which Satan is the Prince, we make our way like lambs among wolves.

On 21 July 1209, the pope's army pitched camp on the banks of the river Orb, below the city. The spiritual leader of the Host was Arnaud-Amaury, abbot of Cîteaux, papal legate. It was his responsibility to preach and encourage the Crusade against the Cathars, including in the court of the king of France. As the army camped beneath the walls of Béziers on the banks of the river Orb, he proclaimed that the city was 'utterly contaminated by heresy' and that even the Catholics who lived there were 'robbers, adulterers, tricksters and deviants'.

A list of 222 names of 'heretics' believed to be living within the city walls was passed to the bishop of Béziers. All but a few of these were *parfaits*, priests of the 'heretic' Cathar church. The Catholic population of the city refused to give them up. Though the Host was vast, the Biterrois were confident in their own defences and the ability of Trencavel to mobilise reinforcements. Whatever engines of war the Crusaders might build and install on the steep slopes below the city wall, they would never match the strength of the fortifications themselves. Unfortunately for the defenders, a devastating mistake in strategy completely undermined their position.

On 22 July 1209, the Feast of St Mary Magdalene, a small party of Biterrois opened a narrow postern gate in the walls and made a sortie. Their overconfidence led them to run towards the river Orb, close to the Crusader camp. They ambushed and killed a French mercenary who climbed up on to the bridge to taunt them and they threw his body into the river. They goaded the soldiers of the Host and some of the hangers-on roused themselves to chase them back up the slope.

Soon the Biterrois realised they had strayed too far from the safety of the walls. Mercenaries among the pope's army, camped nearby, attacked them unexpectedly, throwing them into a panic. The Biterrois scampered desperately up the steep and slippery grass bank towards the postern from which they had emerged. The mercenaries followed on their heels, gaining ground. Some of the Biterrois got inside. Perhaps for fear of abandoning their fellow citizens, perhaps in terror for their own lives, they failed to secure the gate. Some of the mercenaries followed them inside. The defences were breached.

While the rest of the pope's army began to attack the walls with siege engines and scaling ladders, within the walls a massacre had already begun. As word spread of the breach, more and more Crusaders infested the streets. In two to three hours the city was taken, its militias defeated, its people disarmed and hiding in their homes. Systematically, they were dragged out and killed. Many of the citizens of Béziers – Catholics and Cathars together

– rushed through the apocalyptic streets to the cathedral and churches for protection. The Catholic priests who accompanied the Host vested themselves and began to celebrate mass. This was to become a feature of the Crusade against the Cathars – the voices of Catholic clergy raised in pious song as their soldiers slashed and burnt.

On the orders of the abbot of Cîteaux, Arnaud-Amaury, the doors of the Christian sanctuaries were broken in. The people massed in terrified congregation were murdered and their priests struck down as they raised a crucifix or chalice in prayer. Arnaud-Amaury was asked by his troops how they should tell apart the 'heretics' from the 'Catholics'. A German Cistercian monk called Caesar of Heisterbach overheard his reply. The exact translation of the original medieval Latin runs: 'Massacre them, for God knows His own.'

And they did. Historians estimate that 20,000 inhabitants of the city were killed in those few hours. Jubilant, Arnaud-Amaury wrote to his master, Pope Innocent III, presumably expecting praise and approbation: 'The vengeance of God was wonderful – we killed them all!'

Conflict then emerged between the French barons and the *routiers* – mercenaries – and other hangers-on in the vast 200,000-strong crusading mob. For the French and for the Catholic church, the purpose of the Crusade against the Cathars was territorial expansion. The northern barons were – generally – motivated by plunder. But there were some amongst them inflamed by a bloodthirsty missionary zeal that, today, it is surely impossible to comprehend. The pope in Rome wanted mastery of the spiritual life of the region, like a chief executive looking for new markets to exploit.

Arnaud-Amaury claimed that the stupidity of the Biterrois who made the disastrous sortie into the enemy camp, giving up the impregnable citadel, was miraculous evidence of the righteousness of the Crusader cause. Those who murdered the children, women and men of Béziers in God's name still wore the crosses of red cloth on their chests. Despite his sympathy for the Catholic cause, the chronicler Guilhèm of Tudèla reported that the massacre was sinful. But he made no bones about its political and military purpose:

The nobles of France, clergy and laity, princes and marquises, were agreed amongst themselves that whenever a *château*…had to be taken by force, the inhabitants were to be put to the sword and slain; thinking afterwards

A 19th-century woodcut depicting the massacre.

that no man would dare to stand out against them by reason of the fear that would go abroad when it was seen what they had already done.

Another whose missionary zeal would be revealed in his predilection for unthinkable barbarity would step forward at the siege of Carcassonne to take full military control of the Crusade.

That man was Simon of Montfort.

☷ CHAPTER 26 ☷

Montfort

The Crusade against the Cathars lasted from the murder of Peter of Castelnau in 1208 to the pyre at Montségur in 1244. Once the 'safe mountain' had fallen, the structure of the Cathar church was gone. The remaining enclaves could be encircled and besieged at will. The faith of the *Bons Chrétiens* became the exception in Languedoc, rather than the rule. But the story of the Crusade can be divided, with the hindsight of history, into three: the Crusade of the northern barons, the brief Occitan fight back and the Royal Crusade instigated by the French king Louis VIII.

Béziers fell to the northern barons on 22 July 1209. Three days later, the *Ost gran* took Narbonne *en passant* without a fight. On the road northwest towards the Carcassonne gap, the villages were deserted at the rumour of its coming and the mass of soldiers and hangers-on could plunder rations at will. Two days after that, the pope sent Raymond VI of Toulouse a letter congratulating him on joining the Crusade against his own people. On 1 August, the *Ost* saw, for the first time, the walls of the Cité.

On the fortified hill, all was energy and business. Soldiers marched in from Trencavel's vassal *seigneuries* all around, boosting the confidence of the inhabitants, but crowding the narrow streets. The defences were being made ready. At the top of the single circuit of walls – much later a second ring was added – wooden galleries were being built. These were designed to overhang the outside of the walls and were assembled from wood recycled from throughout the Cité, including the pews of the cathedral of Sant-Nasari. Once installed, these galleries – known as *hourds* – gave a vantage for the defenders to fire on enemy sappers below, working literally to undermine the defences or place charges.

Outside the walled city itself, there were three suburbs, two of them also fortified. But the suburbs did not have the additional advantage of rising land. Raymond-Roger Trencavel was concerned for the safety of their inhabitants and proposed an immediate attack on the Crusaders when they came within range of a sortie. Pierre-Roger of Cabaret, a trusted vassal and a powerful military leader in his own right, dissuaded him.

On 3 August, the Crusaders took the suburb of the Bourg and set up their camp on the western bank of the river Aude. They now controlled access to the fresh river water that flowed down to Carcassonne from melting snow high up in the Pyrenees. From this point on the Cité was lost.

The 13th-century carving known as the siege stone is actually thought to depict the Siege of Toulouse but can be seen today by visitors to Carcasonne in the church of Sant Nasari.

Repeated attacks strained the defences. Siege weapons were put into service. Trebuchets and mangonels hurled rocks at and over the walls; scaling parties advanced with their rudimentary ladders; gangs of labourers hurried to fill in the protective ditches, advancing behind heavy wooden mantlets – screens – to protect them from the defenders' fire. Trencavel and his vassals were obliged to ride out and attempt to repel them. The carefully laid provisions were doled out with watchful care. The level of fresh water in the wells began to decline – it was too late to dig them any deeper. The August sun beat down.

One of the fiercest commanders of the Host was Simon of Montfort. He was born around 1165, the same year as the future king of France, Philippe-Auguste, and the same year as the canonisation of Charlemagne. His family seat was in the forest of Yveslines, outside Paris. After the death of his first wife, Montfort's father married Amicie of Leicester and Simon became the heir of her brother, Robert of Leicester. To his eternal frustration and sense of bitter injustice, he would never be allowed to inherit this English earldom.

In 1188, Montfort was present at the meeting between Philippe-Auguste and Henry II of England when they agreed to launch a new Crusade to the Holy Land. Soon after, he married Alix of Montmorency, an extraordinary woman who would become his staunchest ally and, sometimes, surrogate general in the conquest and military domination of Languedoc. They would eventually have seven children, of whom three sons – Simon, Guy and Amaury – would play an important role in the Crusade against the Cathars.

After Henry II's death, Richard the Lionheart took on the English throne, but soon fell out with France. Montfort distinguished himself, routing Richard's troops in 1194 at the siege of Aumale. Five years later,

Richard died and was succeeded by his younger brother, John. In the same year, at a tourna-ment in Champagne, Simon of Montfort and his brother Guy were both persuaded to 'take the cross' and spent much of 1202 and 1203 fight-ing with distinction in the East. Montfort returned in 1204 in time to hear of the death of Robert of Leicester, but King John of England confiscated the property on the pretext that a French-

A 19th-century engraving of Simon of Montfort.

man couldn't be allowed to accede, leaving Montfort with vastly more status than wealth. For this Crusader of conviction, the Crusade against the Cathars was an opportunity to put that right.

A couple of days after Trencavel's sortie, Pedro of Aragon approached Carcassonne in company with a hundred knights. One source says his troop was led to the place by the smoke rising from the already burning stronghold. First, though, he went to a hill set back from the confrontation to speak to Raymond VI of Toulouse, the prevaricating, unwilling Crusader. The meeting of Trencavel's twin lords came to a single conclusion – he must submit. After eating together, Pedro and three of his knights rode to the gates of the Cité and were received with joy. Surely, thought the Carcassonnais, here were the hoped-for reinforcements. But Pedro counselled surrender. Trencavel replied: 'I would rather see every one of my people scorched before my eyes, kiss their corpses and be the last to die.' Pedro abandoned his vassal, his people and his lands and returned across the Pyrenees into Aragon.

On 7 August, another Crusader attack made a breach in the wall of the fortified Castellar suburb, coming close to the walls of the Cité itself. Many fought with clubs against the well-armed Crusader knights. Refugees flooded into the fortified citadel through the Porte de Rodez, swelling a population already struggling with the additional soldiery of Trencavel's vassals. Water was beginning to run short. Minor wounds could – and did – quickly become fatal, filling the streets with the stink of death and corruption. After just a few weeks of siege, the wells had run dry and the city was suffering from siege sickness.

Another embassy came from the Crusaders, this time a knight claiming to be a relative of Trencavel. The offer was doubtless formulated by Arnaud-Amaury, the papal legate who condemned the inhabitants of Béziers to slaughter. It required Trencavel to abandon his people and his Cité and make himself a hostage. Raymond-Roger followed the advice of his liege lord Pedro. On 15 August 1209, the Feast of the Assumption of the Virgin, Raymond-Roger gave himself up to save his people. The Crusaders entered the Cité. Many of the defenders were expelled wearing nothing but 'shirts and braies'. ('Braies' were a kind of loose undergarment like long shorts.)

In contravention of the surrender treaty, Trencavel was imprisoned in a foul dungeon and stripped of his titles. The wealth of Carcassonne was confiscated. Yet Arnaud-Amaury could find no one prepared to take on the viscounty. The lords of Nevers, Bourgogne and Saint-Pol all refused. Why?

Raymond-Roger had been treated treacherously. Philippe-Auguste, the French king, had declined to take part in the Crusade in the first place and its legality was not clear. The main sources of plunder had probably already been sacked. Most importantly, though, these great houses of the north had served their forty days and the bargain struck between the Catholic church and military might of France had been fulfilled.

It is important to remember that, individually, none of the northern houses was more powerful than Toulouse or Aragon. The independence of the south from northern France was well established. Even though the Catholic church attempted to guarantee the property of Crusaders in their absence, this was easier to assert in theory than achieve in practice. The coalition of forces in the Crusade against the Cathars was a fragile one, born of circumstances and self-interest, not conviction, an easier alternative to the arduous and dangerous Crusades to the Holy Land. What was more, Arnaud-Amaury had not consulted Pedro of Aragon on what would happen were Trencavel deposed. The legate had not dared suggest it while Pedro was present. Now, the king of Aragon could not be expected to put up with unilateral changes in the lands of his vassals without conflict, even if the weak-willed Raymond VI of Toulouse had no stomach for the fight.

Nevertheless, Arnaud-Amaury knew he needed a general to manage in the field, to pacify the country now its figurehead had been struck off. He looked about him at the assembled lords, some itching to be gone, some sated by victory, some tempted by further murderous exploits in the name of Christian charity. He judged well when he offered the role to a Crusader zealot, a veteran of Crusades to the East, a man of significant valour in the siege of Carcassonne and characterised by obscene self-righteousness. Yet the viscounty was clearly viewed as such a poisoned pill that even this 'soldier of Christ' turned down the first proposal. Perhaps he was then shown that he could not refuse and Simon of Montfort was named viscount of Béziers and Carcassonne.

Contemporary descriptions portray Montfort as a mighty figure, tall, heavily built with a mass of dark brown hair and substantial beard. He was already in his forties by the time of the Crusade against the Cathars, almost old age for the medieval period, a man of severe morals with a highly judgemental cast of mind. His devotion to his principles and his bravery in battle won him the respect and trust of his soldiers. The remarkable success of his strategies – even when outflanked or outnumbered – must have given confidence to his troops.

After the fall of Carcassonne, Montfort embarked on a combination of steady siege and rapid guerrilla warfare. He was, in the words of one historian, 'everywhere at once', indefatigable and determined. His progress, today, can be followed across Languedoc by the trail of monuments to his victims.

CHAPTER 27

The *Canso* of Guilhèm of Tudèla

*A*fter the fall of Carcassonne, the Crusade was led by Simon of Montfort. Every stronghold and every village he subdued satisfied his self-righteous malice and increased his wealth. The story was recorded in a song, an epic poem, *La Canso de la Crosada*.

The *Canso* was written in Occitan, nearly 10,000 lines of rhyming verse, a traditional way of telling stories at a time when books were rare, when being caught in possession of a copy of St John's Gospel in *langue d'oc* would almost certainly lead to imprisonment.

The text of the *Canso* was, for many years, lost. The sole manuscript copy of the poem that has survived was written out around 1275, more than fifty years after the original was composed. The text comprises 120 sheets of vellum, a precious writing material cut from the skin of stillborn calves. Both sides of each sheet are used, covered in a text written in a Gothic hand. The first letters are illuminated in red and blue in an alternating sequence. The text is illustrated with thirteen drawings which – no one knows why – were not coloured in.

The first historical record of the existence of this text of the *Canso* appeared in 1337, in the property records of an inhabitant of the Quercy region, north of Toulouse. Then there is a gap until it is listed among the belongings of Cardinal Mazarin, an Italian diplomat and churchman who served the French monarchy in the mid-17th century. In the following century, it passed through the hands of two of Louis XV's noblemen, then, in 1780, found its way into the king's library. Following the Revolution in 1789, the text was transferred to the Bibliothèque Nationale, but still it went unnoticed – a long and difficult poem of nearly 9,600 polysyllabic lines in the fading, almost forgotten language of the southwest.

At this time, there were only three texts of any note concerning the

Crusade against the Cathars in the public domain. The first two were 13th-century Latin histories, one of which was written by Pierre of Les Vaux-de-Cernay, a Cistercian monk who joined the Crusade with his uncle, the abbot of Les Vaux-de-Cernay, who had close ties with Simon of Montfort. His *Historia Albigensis* is the main reason why the Crusade came to be known by the rather misleading title of Albigensian Crusade. It is also the origin of the term *perfectus* – 'perfected one' – for a Cathar priest and the earliest indication that they wore black robes.

The third text was a rather disappointing prose work, written in the Toulouse dialect of Occitan, in the 15th century. In 1837, an academic from the Sorbonne in Paris published the Bibliothèque Nationale's manuscript 25425 – *La Canso de la Crosada* – and it immediately became apparent that the disappointing prose text in *toulousain* was merely a poor summary of Tudèla's epic poem. Further study revealed two authors, both of whom were directly involved in the events themselves. This was an extraordinary discovery.

The author of the first part of the *Canso*, Guilhèm of Tudèla, was a well-read cleric who announced his own name at the beginning of the poem, as was often the case. He cites other works of medieval epic poetry as his model, including the *Song of Roland*, based on the life of Charlemagne, and the *Song of Antioch*, based on events in the Crusades to the Holy Land. In 1200, Guilhèm was present at the marriage of Raymond VI of Toulouse to Eleanor of Aragon. Soon after the beginning of the Crusade against the Cathars, he went to live in the *château* of Bruniquel on the river Aveyron, north of Carcassonne. This castle on the pilgrim route to Santiago de Compostela was a gift from Raymond VI of Toulouse to his traitorous younger brother, Baldwin. Guilhèm became unofficial scribe to Baldwin's treachery.

When the Crusade against the Cathars came south, opposition could come from three main sources: the house of Toulouse, the house of Trencavel and the house of Aragon. All three domains were related by family and in feudal relationships equivalent to treaties of common defence. Of course, the goals of the Crusaders – wiping out the Cathar church and plundering land and wealth – could more easily be achieved if the three houses were split one from another. It could be even more advantageous if a split could come about within the family of one of the potential allies. So it transpired.

Raymond V of Toulouse lived to sixty years old and had four children. At his death in 1194, his eldest son – also Raymond – inherited virtually all his wealth plus the title of sixth count Raymond of Toulouse. Raymond V's daughter, Adélaïde, married Roger Trencavel II, father of Raymond-Roger Trencavel, who was deserted by Aragon and Toulouse at the siege of Carcassonne in 1209. Raymond V's youngest child, Baldwin, received a meagre inheritance portion but made up for it with cartloads of resentment. Even the gift of the château of Bruniquel that he received from his brother, Raymond VI, could not mollify him.

In 1209, under threat of excommunication, Raymond VI decided – quite literally – to pitch his tent in the camp of the Crusaders. But he did not take arms against the people of Languedoc. Baldwin, on the other hand, entered into an alliance with Simon of Montfort and made himself a servant of the Crusade. In May 1210, the spring that followed the fall of Carcassonne, Guilhèm of Tudèla claims that he embarked on the *Canso*, beginning with the assassination of the papal legate Castelnau and Pope Innocent III's call to arms.

It only took Guilhèm a few hundred lines to tell the 'story so far'. He described the cross made of red cloth that adorned the Crusaders' clothing. He wrote of the 'long serpent of weapons' snaking south to the gates of Béziers. He introduced the figure of Raymond-Roger Trencavel, the twenty-four-year-old nephew of Raymond VI: 'He loved with all his heart all the people of all the lands of which he was lord. His people had for him neither distrust nor fear. They behaved with him like brothers and sisters.'

Guilhèm described Trencavel's departure from Béziers, accompanied by the Jews of the city, the massacre of the Biterrois, then the siege and surrender of the impregnable fortress Cité of Carcassonne. Of Trencavel's surrender to Montfort, he astutely wrote: 'He gave himself up as a hostage of his own free will. And it was great madness, in my opinion, to have handed himself over in this way.'

Sure enough, imprisoned in his own dungeon, Trencavel was soon dead and Montfort lord of the Cité. The *Canso* then tells the tale of Montfort's 'pacification' of Languedoc, the battles, skirmishes, pyres and scaffolds. From about 1212 there is no doubt that Guilhèm was virtually writing the *Canso* as it unfolded before his astonished eyes.

As a Catholic cleric, Guilhèm was obliged to support the Crusade. He wrote panegyrics to Montfort and to his master Baldwin. He described Catharism as 'execrable madness', the Cathars themselves as 'unbelieving people' who had lost 'the way'. However, even though he knew that the vast majority of the people of Languedoc opposed the Crusade, he didn't condemn them outright. In fact, he sympathised with some of the catastrophes they suffered.

In February 1214, men loyal to Toulouse captured Baldwin. Raymond VI, his elder brother, unsurprisingly hanged him for treason. It may be that Guilhèm was also killed at this point or, perhaps, he had been taken prisoner the previous summer when the *Canso* abruptly broke off. It seems certain that he didn't survive. Perhaps he should have heeded his own advice for those caught in the path of the Crusade. He recommended turning away and sheltering from the storm: 'Only a madman would try to resist.'

Or perhaps, as an eyewitness to the barbarity of Montfort's 'pacification' of Languedoc, it is tempting to believe that Guilhèm had become sickened by what he saw. Another 12th-century 'heretic' Christian, a member of the Vaudois sect from Lyon, put it succinctly: 'Between persecutors and persecuted, the Christians are always the persecuted.'

⚏ CHAPTER 28 ⚏

'Pacification'

*M*ontfort's first objective was to quell resistance, to pacify the land.

In the 13th century, there was no word for Languedoc, but those who lived there were, as Raymond VII of Toulouse put it, the 'people of our language'. And the Crusaders – the *Militia Christi* – were invaders, a foreign army: French, Flemish, Rhinelanders, Bavarians, English, Scottish and even Austrian.

Despite what many people say, it is hard to find a truly untranslatable word, but *paratge* may just be one. It refers to a set of values and a code of behaviour native to the Midi. *Paratge* means equality, generosity, love, honour, loyalty and pleasure, imbued with a sense of optimism or improvement. It is the foundation on which the *trobadors* of Languedoc first developed the notions of chivalry and courtesy that we associate with a noble tradition of medieval honour and justice.

Concepts of fair play in battle and respect for one's opponent – as in the tale of Charlemagne's siege of Carcassonne – were a feature of the epic poems of the period. In Languedoc, as well as tales of war, tales of love entertained the court, poems and songs in which a worthy knight expressed *fin'amor* – courtly love – for his chosen lady.

A key element of *fin'amor* was devotion, generally of a knight of inferior social status to a higher-ranked lady. In its purest form, the devotion was expressed innocently, hopelessly, with the knight acknowledging that his love had no chance of ever being rewarded. Because the lady was unattainable, the knight's valour and selflessness would increase and he would become capable of acts of the most extraordinary bravery and – ultimately – self-sacrifice. If ever there was a possibility that the distant and disinterested lady might come to respond to his yearning, disaster – as in the

The ruins that tourists visit today are much higher up the ridge.

case of Lancelot and Guinevere – would doubtless ensue.

At the beginning of the 12th century, Raymond of Miraval was one of the best-known *trobadors* of all Languedoc. Raymond was *co-seigneur* of a small *château* in the Cabardès region of the Montagne Noire and a personal friend of Raymond VI of Toulouse. He wrote verse in praise of courtly love, Raymond-Roger Trencavel and his country, as well as works of love for his *Mais d'Amic* – his 'more than friend' – the unattainable wife of one of the *seigneurs* of Cabaret.

In fact, at the siege of Carcassonne, one of Trencavel's staunchest allies in the defence of Carcassonne was Pierre-Roger of Cabaret, *seigneur* of the place now called Lastours – the towers. When the Cité surrendered in 1209, many of the defenders fled to his stronghold north of Carcassonne in the Cabardès hills.

For generations, Cabaret had been a haven for Cathars, for *trobadors* and the nobility of the *langue d'oc* – in short, for *paratge*. Like many of the castles roundabout, the first evidence of its occupation comes from at least 1,500 years BCE. It was fortified in the Roman era, then, when Rome fell, the Christian Visigoths occupied it.

The location is a rocky ridge about 300 metres long, the valleys either side carved out by two rivers, the torrent of the Grésilhou to the west and the more substantial Orbiel to the east. At the southern end of the ridge, the two rivers merged into a single course – the Orbiel – and flowed down to join the Aude at Trèbes, east of the Cité. Archaeological excavations have shown that, in the time of the Crusade against the Cathars, there were three *castra* – fortified villages – on the western side of the ridge, between the Grésilhou and the steeply rising land. Each was made up of a cluster of houses – grouped round a single tall tower, a blacksmith's forge and several rainwater reservoirs.

The road to Carcassonne – no more than a path at the time of the Crusade, too narrow for carts or siege engines – was on the far western side of the Grésilhou. The sloping land roundabout was cultivated using terraces. The relatively reliable flow of the Orbiel to the east of the ridge provided power for at least two watermills.

The northern *castrum* huddled round the home of Pierre-Roger, the *tour* Cabaret, in a series of semicircular terraces, the houses attached to one another to provide defensive security. The middle *castrum* – Surdespine – was the smallest, tucked into a fold of the ridge, just a dozen buildings. The largest – numbering perhaps 120 dwellings – was at the southern end. Again, the houses were built into terraces or joined together with fortifications and clustered round the tall tower of Quertinheux, not far from the cave called the *trou de la Cité*. All the towers of Lastours had extensive underground chambers and legend says that this 'hole' was the entrance to an underground passage linking the citadel of Lastours with Carcassonne itself. If so, the route is unknown.

Above the northernmost tower of Cabaret, on the ridge itself, was a lookout tower, dominating views up into the hills of Cabardès. Another lookout was in the middle of the ridge at its highest point – about 300 metres above sea level, above the smallest middle *castrum*. From here the sentries could observe the land unimpeded in all directions. The southern end of the ridge relied on the tall Quertinheux tower for protection.

Montfort was wary of Lastours. He thought – rightly – that it was an immensely strong defensive position. In September 1209, just a month after the surrender of the Cité, a Crusader force followed the valley of the Orbiel into the hills and attempted to storm the *castra*. Pierre-Roger and his men easily repelled the attack. A few months later, a Crusader expedition of about fifty men was routed by the knights of Cabaret. The *châteaux* became a centre of resistance and refuge, and Montfort looked for easier targets on the plains.

The winter was no time for campaigning. In early spring of 1210, the troops of Simon of Montfort put down a rebellion in Montlaur, between Carcassonne and Trèbes, but failed to catch the leaders, Olivier of Montlaur and Chabert of Barbaira. Those he did catch were hanged. Later that same March, when he turned his mind to Bram, Montfort had clearly decided that hanging was insufficient deterrent for those unwilling to accept forced conversion to the Catholic faith.

Two thousand years ago, Bram was a small – but important – town on the road northwest from Carcassonne towards Aquitaine. The Romans called it Vicus Eburomagnus. (In Latin, *'vicus'* was a settlement that grew up spontaneously around some official Roman site – in this case, it seems, a wine market.) Of course, where there was trade, the Romans built roads. In the case of Bram, traces of the Via Aquitania – the road to Bordeaux and the Atlantic – can still be seen today. And where there was wine, there were potters. The remains of two potteries from the reign of Augustus at the turn of the first Christian millennium have also been uncovered. The site was perhaps abandoned after the departure of the Romans.

Seen, today, from a plane approaching Carcassonne from the northwest, the centre of modern Bram is almost perfectly circular, the houses arranged in concentric terraces, an archetypal Languedoc *circulade*. It is about halfway between Carcassonne and Castelnaudary, surrounded by flat, fertile land. In the 12th century, the river Preuilhe was channelled into the moat of the castle, but no trace of the fortification remains. Around the time of the Crusade against the Cathars, the town numbered about 240 *foyers* – 'hearths' or 'households'.

Bram had a large population of Cathars and was defended by a garrison loyal to the 'heretics'. Montfort's forces approached, in company with a Spanish Catholic evangelist called Domingo de Guzmán. The *castrum* was surrounded and a three-day siege ended in the capitulation of the defenders. Montfort took more than a hundred prisoners. He ordered his men to cut off their ears, their noses and their top lips. Then he commanded that all but one should have his eyes put out. The last should be blinded in just one eye so that he could lead the miserable parade in single file across country to Cabaret, each man's right hand on the shoulder of the one in front, an example to all of the folly of opposing the 'soldiers of Christ'.

The following month, Montfort besieged the *château* of Chabert of Barbaira – also known as Miramont and, confusingly, Alaric. It was a fortnight before it fell. The April weather was dreadful and made the attack difficult. The Crusaders lost a number of important leaders but, finally, took the stronghold. Also in April, an attack on Cabaret was repelled. Then Montfort visited Pamiers, where Pedro of Aragon had organised diplomatic talks with Raymond VI of Toulouse and Raymond-Roger of Foix, the Pyrenean enclave. Nothing came immediately of the discussions, but Pedro didn't give up. After more meetings with Foix, with Raymond of Termes and Aimery of Montréal, he managed to persuade Montfort to sign up to a limited ceasefire before returning across the Pyrenees into Spain.

Despite his good intentions, Pedro probably played into Montfort's hands. The weather was not, at that time, on the Crusaders' side. To crack the defences of the citadels of Languedoc, Montfort needed the long hot days of summer. He marked time until June, when he launched a decisive conflict at Minerve.

⌘ CHAPTER 29 ⌘

Minerve

uisserguier is a medieval *circulade* built of concentric rings of houses round a central *château*, around halfway between Béziers and Narbonne. The castle was built in the 11th and 12th centuries in grey local stone. If you look carefully, you can still see the damage inflicted during the Crusade against the Cathars. It is surrounded by vines whose wines were once served in Julius Caesar's Rome.

Puisserguier would be just another 'heretic' village were it not for the actions of Guiraud of Pépieux, a treacherous local *seigneur* who had taken the cross and fought against Trencavel at the siege of Carcassonne. That was in August 1209, a long hot summer. By November the weather had turned wet and miserable, Raymond-Roger Trencavel was dead and Guiraud had a grievance. His uncle had been murdered by one of Montfort's companions. Although the murderer was punished by being buried alive, Guiraud deserted Montfort and, with a few of his friends and surprise on his side, overpowered and imprisoned the fifty-strong garrison at Puisserguier. Montfort reacted swiftly, asking the Narbonne militia to retake the stronghold, but they refused. Montfort marched on the village himself and Guiraud panicked. He threw the defending garrison into the moat and set fire to the castle. He escaped across country to the citadel of Minerve, 35 kilometres away. He took with him the two knights who had commanded Puisserguier, before beating them and setting them naked on the road to rejoin Montfort.

In June of the following year, Guiraud of Pépieux was a trusted soldier in the forces of Guillaume of Minerve. Guillaume was lord of yet another supposedly impregnable Languedoc fortress. The town stood on a triangular promontory of rock protected by 50-metre-deep gorges cut by the rivers Cesse and Brian. Inhabited since the Stone Age, Minerve was named by the soldiers of the Roman 10th Legion after Minerva, their goddess of war. Pliny the Elder admired the wines of the Minervois, grown on the gently sloping hills round about. The church of Saint-Etienne houses a white marble altar from the middle of the 5th century, after the fall of the Roman Empire, covered with hundreds of Christian Visigoth signatures.

Minerve today.

Guillaume, the lord of Minerve, was typical of the nobility of Languedoc, a man of *paratge*. He appreciated poetry and song. His wife, Rixovenda of Termes, was a popular feminine idol in the verse of the *trobadors*. He was closely allied to Trencavel and to Pierre-Roger of Cabaret, another fortress town north of Carcassonne. At his own expense he housed groups of Cathar priests, who had fled Béziers before the massacre, in the road now called the rue des Martyrs.

In early June 1210, it was Guiraud of Pépieux whose reconnaissance party brought Guillaume word that a Crusader army was approaching. Intelligence revealed that Montfort had recently received reinforcements from throughout France and even Germany. But Montfort had to move quickly – the new Crusaders would only give him forty days' service before returning to their homes secure in the knowledge that their efforts had won them absolution.

Guillaume of Minerve was confident that he could resist long enough for Montfort's army to disperse. He – like pretty much all the military strategists of the period – believed that defence was always stronger than attack. It seems strange that the lessons of Béziers and Carcassonne – surely so vivid in the memory – should not yet have been learnt. True, Pierre-

Roger of Cabaret had repelled a small-scale attack on his *castra* at Lastours, but Guiraud of Pépieux knew Montfort's methods at first hand. He fled Minerve, as he had fled Puisserguier. He became captain of a guerrilla force fighting for Raymond of Toulouse against Montfort. (He survived for thirty years until he was finally hanged by the army of the king of France in 1240.)

Around the middle of June 1210, the Crusader force was encamped on the flat land above the gorges. They did not dare go down into the canyons for fear of becoming trapped. They may have already discovered that the sides of the river gorges were perforated by caves and overhangs where defenders were hidden. Montfort pitched his tent to the east of the citadel. He examined the defences and declared: 'The *château* of Minerve...is built on a high hill. Between here and Spain there is no better defended castle, except Cabaret and Termes.'

The additional advantage at Cabaret was that there were no vantages from which to attack the high ground on which the *castra* were built, because the flat land east and west was well below the level of the ridge. At Minerve, though, the steep gorges rose quickly to allow the attackers to look the defender in the eye across the void.

So it would, once more, come down to a blockade. The army split into four and established siege weapons north, south, east and west. It was common in medieval warfare to give names to these awesome rock-launchers. The largest of the four – erected by Montfort's camp in the east – was so impressive that its name has been recorded by history: *Mala Vezina* or *Malvoisine* – the 'Neighbour From Hell'.

Local knowledge should have been all on the side of the 'people of our language' – of the *langue d'oc*. But Montfort discovered that the only source of water was a covered well at the foot of one of the gorges. The *Mala Vezina* was erected above it and quickly demolished both the stair that led down from the town and the well machinery. On 27 June, a squad of defenders crept out armed with straw, dry faggots and cooking grease. They clambered down into the gorge, then hauled themselves up and out on the meagre vegetation that grew in crevices in the rock. They cut the throats of perhaps two Crusader sentries and stacked their portable bonfire round the base of the *Mala Vezina*. But before the fire could properly take, a sentry they had missed – because he had wandered off to defecate – raised the alarm and they had to retreat in desperation. The darkness of the night allowed them to make it back to the walls.

The *Mala Vezina* was saved and continued launching great lumps of rock

– weighing as much as 200 kilograms – across the canyon. Little by little, it gnawed chunks from the thick fortified walls and stove in the fragile roofs. The sun shone through the holes. The summer of 1210 was just as hot and dry as the previous year when the defenders of Carcassonne were conquered by sickness and thirst. Death became a fact of life in the besieged citadel. The rocky outcrop on which the town was built had no deep soil that could be dug for graves. Bodies were tossed over the walls into the ravines to rot and the summer fragrances of pine and lavender were overwhelmed by the stink of rotting flesh.

The siege followed its inexorable course. After seven weeks, around 20 July, the limit of the Crusader reinforcements' forty days, Guillaume of Minerve left his stronghold. He and Montfort began to negotiate the terms of surrender, but were interrupted by the papal legates. One of them was Arnaud-Amaury, abbot of Cîteaux, spiritual leader of the Crusade against the Cathars, the man who instructed the 'soldiers of Christ' to massacre the entire population of Béziers. He commanded: 'Minerve will become the property of the leader of the Crusade [Montfort], but the inhabitants will be allowed to live, even the *parfaits* and *parfaites*, providing they abjure their faith.'

One of Montfort's commanders complained at this generosity. The abbot replied: 'Don't worry. You will see that very few of them will convert.'

Despite the abbot's bad faith, several members of the Crusader force tried to persuade the inhabitants of the fallen stronghold to embrace Catholicism. The only one who was successful was an elderly woman called Mathilde de Garlande, who travelled with the army as a friend of Montfort's wife, Alix. She convinced three Cathars to abjure. Meanwhile, on 22 July, the Crusader army marched across the natural stone bridge into the citadel. The monks chanted the *Te Deum* as a pyre was built at the foot of the gorge of the Cesse. Over 140 *parfaits* and *parfaites* were hurled from the walls into the ravine. The Cistercian chronicler Pierre of Les Vaux-de-Cernay wrote that the Cathars went 'voluntarily' into the flames, asserting 'Neither death nor life can separate us from the faith to which we are joined.'

Guillaume committed himself to serve Montfort and, in compensation for his lost citadel, was given land near Béziers. (Six years later, he changed sides once more and joined the forces of Raymond the Younger of Toulouse – the future Raymond VII. In 1219, he fought for Raymond against Louis VIII of France at the siege of Toulouse.) The Crusaders set light to all their temporary shelters and stores of wood, lighting up the valley so it could be seen for miles around. Understanding that Minerve had fallen, Aimery of Montréal immediately sent a delegation of surrender and swapped his hill fortress for land on the plain. The lord of Laurac did much the same.

In 1982, the massacre of the Cathars of Minerve was commemorated with a sculpture created by Jean-Luc Severac. It is a large piece of dark grey rock into which has been cut the shape of a dove. It is dedicated by the addition of the Occitan

'They trusted only in the Word'

words '*Als Catars*' – 'To the Cathars'. Severac says that he cut the shape of the dove in the rock because 'The Cathars raised themselves above the material world...so I made the dove not of stone but of light. Light – the absence of matter – is the only appropriate way to represent Catharism.'

CHAPTER 30
Termes

fter the fall of Minerve, Montfort regrouped. He and his commanders decided the next major target should be the *château* of Termes, one of five mountain strongholds known as the *cinq fils de Carcassonne* – the five sons – along with Aguilar, Quéribus, Peyrepertuse and Puilaurens.

Termes is the closest to the Cité, 28 kilometres to the southeast and 460 metres above sea level, capital of the land known as Termenès. Even today, there is no fast road, the way sliding alongside the water in gorges cut by rivers, skirting the peaks. The modern village of Termes, which nestles in a fold of land beneath the *château* where the Crusaders exiled it, is home to only about sixty people. In the time of the Crusade, the *castrum* nestled against the walls of the *château*.

One route south from Carcassonne goes through Ladern-sur-Lauquet, where, around the Feast of St Louis

In 1653, the château at Termes was the impregnable headquarters of a gang of highwaymen and bandits, so the French king had it destroyed with explosives. This cruciform window survived.

on 25 August, an extraordinary annual carnival takes place. Through the narrow rustic streets, a band of local people leads a procession. A cart carries a fool, fishing with a carrot carved like a phallus. To kiss the phallus will bring fertility and good luck. In the evening, the *bal* is interrupted by a gang of Languedocien pantaloons, draped in ludicrous nightgowns, their faces daubed white with flour. These are the *bufòlis*, just one element of a festival that has its roots in the pagan Dark Ages.

Travelling by a different road, Termes can be approached via Lagrasse, where an abbey was first built before the time of Charlemagne. Most of what can be seen today was built more recently, but the south transept dates from the 11th century, the time of the first public burnings of Cathars. It wouldn't be many years before the lords of the *château* at Termes came into conflict with the clerics at Lagrasse.

In the second half of the 12th century, the *seigneurs* of Termes reopened the region's iron and silver mines. With the revenue, they began to build *castra* to house their lesser nobility and people. The lands on which they built these *castra* were disputed by the Lagrasse abbey, whose response was to excommunicate the lords of Termes, not once but several times. Apart from this theoretical punishment, the abbey was impotent. The *castra* were garrisoned with knights loyal to the lords of Termes and, perhaps more importantly, it was at this same period that the household converted to the religion of the *Bons Chrétiens*.

Militarily, Termes was secure. By 1207 Raymond of Termes was lord of the citadel and perhaps sixty villages round about. Spiritually, their salvation was in their own hands, not those of the opulent, intolerant Catholic clerics. Raymond's brother, Benoît of Termes, a Cathar *parfait*, was sent as a representative of the Cathar church to a debate with Catholic theologians at Montréal. The Cathars asserted baldly that only they – and not the church in Rome – had the power to save souls. But the world turned and the balance of power in Languedoc changed.

Before Montfort could attack the fortress, a substantial quantity of siege engines had to be assembled. The weapons were brought to Carcassonne in pieces and stocked. Intelligence got out and 300 men of Cabaret walked through the night to the Cité and attempted to burn them, but the defenders got the better of them. The weapons were loaded on to carts and dragged nearly 30 kilometres through the countryside on unmade roads to the foot of the hill. By August 1210 the blockade was in place.

The battle for Termes began in August 1210 with an exchange of fire from siege weapons. The castle was well defended by about fifty knights garrisoned behind its thick, high walls. Bizarrely, the Catholic bishop of Carcassonne was in the Crusader encampment while, behind the walls, his brother fought alongside the knights of Raymond of Termes.

An attack on the south flank of the mountain, led by Simon of Montfort himself, was repulsed. A new assault was made on an outcrop known as the Termenet and the defenders' small garrison was dislodged. Montfort had siege weapons brought up to the Termenet and began a new bombardment of the *château*. Meanwhile, Pierre-Roger of Cabaret sent men to intercept Montfort's supply columns and cut down the Crusader rearguard. The men Pierre-Roger captured were mutilated in revenge for the atrocity ordered by Montfort at Bram.

Summer dragged on. In September, Raymond of Termes, the lord of the *château*, agreed to a treaty of surrender, but then abandoned it when an abrupt period of rain replenished the empty reservoirs. By November, despite the absence of any substantial military breakthrough, the situation was desperate once more. Under cover of night on the 22 and 23 of the month, most of the defenders of the fortress slipped away, tired, hungry and ravaged by dysentery from the exhausted wells and *citernes*. Raymond of Termes was among them, then he changed his mind and slipped back into the castle, declining to abandon his citadel. He was arrested by Montfort's troops the following day. He later died in the prison at Carcassonne.

Montfort was delighted with his triumph. He marched on Coustaussa and found it abandoned. The Cathar *castrum* at Albedun surrendered and a three-day siege sufficed to take the *château* of Puivert. His only significant failure of the entire year was Cabaret. Wisely, Montfort decided to wait out the winter before his next major campaign.

⚏ CHAPTER 31 ⚏

Lavaur

t the beginning of 1211, eighteen months after the fall of Carcassonne, everything hung in the balance. Montfort's troops had little continuity, except for those commanders to whom he awarded conquered territories. New 'soldiers of Christ' were urgently needed for the campaign season that would come with improved weather. To assist Montfort, Bishop Foulques of Toulouse went north into the lands of the French king Philippe-Auguste to preach the Crusade against the Cathars once more. The French king wrote to the pope to complain.

The previous year, in Toulouse, Bishop Foulques had set up the *Confrérie Blanche* – the White Brotherhood – a Catholic militia whose goal was to terrorise 'heretics' and their protectors, including Raymond VI. The *Confrérie* was drawn mainly from the population of the city centre. In response Raymond set up his own *Confrérie Noire*, drawn almost entirely from the suburbs. The *Canso* considered Foulques a traitor to Toulouse and called him the 'bishop of devils' and the 'criminal bishop' for stirring up civil war.

Meanwhile, Pierre-Roger of Cabaret received intelligence that Montfort was planning a full-out attack on his *castrum*. He decided his situation was hopeless. He released a Crusader prisoner, Bouchard of Marly, and sent him on his way, dressed in new clothes with a 'fine-stepping steed' accompanied by 'three well-turned-out pages'. Bouchard provided the necessary intermediary for surrender to be negotiated. Delighted to have taken possession of the fortress without loss of men or equipment, Montfort turned his attention to Lavaur, 15 kilometres northeast of Toulouse.

In the 12th century, Lavaur was on the border of the domains of Toulouse and Trencavel. By 1178 the town was the seat of the Cathar bishop of

Toulouse and prominent believers were given safe passage from the city to attend a debate with Catholics in Toulouse. Unfortunately, the Catholics didn't understand much *langue d'oc* and the Cathars didn't speak medieval Latin. In 1181, a small armed force accompanying a legate was let into the town by the wife of Roger II Trencavel, who happened to be present. The Catholic legate harangued another pair of Cathars who, incredibly, renounced the faith of a lifetime and, shortly after, took up posts as Catholic canons in Toulouse. Perhaps the whole episode was set up in advance.

In their later justifications for the atrocities of the Crusade against the Cathars, Catholics referred to Lavaur as 'the very seat of Satan and capital of heresy'. In 1211, at least 300, perhaps 400 *Bons Chrétiens* – *parfaits* and *parfaites* – lived peaceably, openly in Lavaur. Many of them worked, combing wool or making clothes, their low houses open on to the narrow streets. Their humility and their blessings were a comfort to their neighbours. Some were refugees from the towns and villages already conquered by Montfort's army. The town was also home to a number of *faydits* – dispossessed knights – and Aimery of Montréal, the man-mountain leader of the garrison, had at least eighty men at his command. The lady of Lavaur was Guiraude, Aimery's sister, an elderly, strong-willed Cathar of noble Languedoc lineage.

The siege of the town began in April 1211. Montfort expected to receive reinforcements at any moment, in particular a column of German Crusaders. Foulques of Toulouse sent him 5,000 volunteers from his *Confrérie Blanche* militia and Raymond VI of Toulouse in person joined the defenders with a handful of knights. The ceasefire brokered by Pedro of Aragon with Raymond-Roger of Foix, the Pyrenean enclave, came to an end. Raymond-Roger, seething with pent-up frustration at having left Montfort *carte blanche* for so long, ambushed the disorganised column of 5,000 Germans and massacred the entire company. One of his captains was Guiraud of Pépieux, the man who briefly defied Montfort at Puisserguier before becoming a *faydit* – a dispossessed knight – of the guerrilla resistance.

After more than a month of siege, in May 1211, the Crusaders managed to advance a *chatte* – a protective shelter – close to the fortifications. A party of engineers undermined the wall and made a breach. Dame Guiraude, lady of Lavaur – an old woman by medieval standards – was lifted up bodily, carried out of the town and, still alive, thrown down a well. Stones were then dropped down on top of her until she no longer cried out. The author of the *Canso* condemned the soldiers 'for never did a living soul leave her roof without having eaten well first'.

The lady's brother, Aimery of Montréal, was forced up on to a scaffold to be hanged, but the gibbet collapsed under his weight. Montfort ordered his men to cut his throat and do the same to all his eighty knights. Next, the 'soldiers of Christ' and a crowd of zealous Catholic pilgrims burnt alive the 300 or 400 Cathars on the largest communal pyre of the entire Crusade. Then they looted the town, the largest collection of booty since Carcassonne.

Soon after, Montfort besieged the *castrum* of Les Cassès, home of the well-known *Bonne Chrétienne* Alazaïs of Roqueville, whose son Raymond was *seigneur*. The siege soon ended with the capitulation of the defenders. None of the Cathars who had taken refuge in the *tour* would abjure, so sixty more souls 'made a good end' on a communal pyre. (Alazaïs seems to have escaped and lived under cover until 1240.) After Les Cassès, the Crusader army moved on, with equal 'success', to Montferrand and then Avignonet.

The mass burnings of Lavaur and Les Cassès seem to have marked a turning point in the Crusade against the Cathars. The strategy of Montfort's campaign remained the same – summer sieges and exemplary punishments – but the Cathar priests themselves became harder to find. Less and less, they put their faith in fortified citadels. More and more, they trusted to their wits and the assistance of the faithful. Increasing numbers lived in secret outside the towns and villages, itinerant yet coming when called, walking the well-trodden pathways more often by night than by day, sleeping in safe hovels in the woods of the Montagne Noire, the Corbières and – finally – the Pyrenees.

⚎ CHAPTER 32 ⚎

Pedro of Aragon

*P*edro of Aragon was born in the mid-1170s. As well as his title of king of Aragon, he was also count of Barcelona and marquis of Provence. His family was entangled through marriage and feudal fealty with those of Trencavel and Toulouse. Through his trans-Pyrenean court, Pedro contributed to the expansion of Occitan poetry and song in Catalonia.

In 1204, in order to extend his domains in southern France, he married Marie of Montpellier, half-sister of Agnès of Montpellier, wife of Raymond-Roger Trencavel. In the same year, he had himself crowned in Rome by Pope Innocent III and took a vow to defend the Catholic faith, so he is known to history in his own tongue as Pere II el Catòlic.

The consuls of Montpellier were aware that Pedro felt no real affection for Marie. Concerned there might not be an heir, they told Pedro that a young widow to whom he was attracted would come to his bed after dark. The king was delighted and bought the subterfuge. Of course, the woman sent to his chamber that

Pedro arranged to be crowned by Innocent III – his Catholicism was political as well as spiritual.

night was Marie. When Pedro discovered this the following morning, he does not seem to have been disappointed and Marie in due course bore him a son, James. By 1210, however, Pedro was trying to persuade the pope to annul his marriage. Concerned for her own future and that of her son, Marie went to Rome to plead her cause.

Probably while she was away in Rome, Montfort took James hostage in Carcassonne. In 1211, Pedro's sister Sanchia married Raymond the Younger of Toulouse, the future Raymond VII. Meanwhile Pedro was occupied with preparations for conflict with the Moors in Spain.

At the beginning of 1212, the Moors were united in a territory that spread all across the Maghreb in North Africa and the width of the southern Iberian Peninsula. The fragmented Catholic kingdoms of Spain were anything but united. The king of Castile asked Pope Innocent III to call for a Crusade to be launched against the Muslims, to which Pedro contributed 50,000 men. The conflict ebbed and flowed until, finally, decisive battle was joined at Las Navas de Tolosa.

At dawn on the morning of Monday 16 July 1212, having been to confession and received communion, the Catholic forces lined up against 200,000 Muslim troops. The battle started badly, with the Christians losing men and ground on both flanks, and some began to desert. In response, several charges were launched by the Catholic leaders, breaking the Muslim lines and fighting their way to the ranks of archers. Under the pressure of the assault, the Muslims began to fall back in disarray and, finally, the Muslim general fled the field and the Catholic triumph was complete. Amidst the bodies of the dead, the Crusaders came together to pray and give thanks. The archbishop of Toledo led the soldiers in singing the *Te Deum* as the blood soaked into the soil.

Pedro was a hero. As the year turned, he was given papal immunity from excommunication and, for the people of Languedoc, 1213 began with a faint whisper of hope.

Pope Innocent III had come to realise that Montfort was as much a danger to the Catholic project as its most potent weapon. At each step in Montfort's barbaric campaign to eradicate 'heresy', his cruel strategies reinforced the people's respect for the *Bons Chrétiens*. Innocent gave the order to end the Crusade. He wrote to Montfort to remind him that his mission was to rid the lands of 'heretics', not to take over those lands himself: 'You have used the army of Crusaders to spill the blood of the just, you have wounded the innocent.'

The pope also had word of how his placemen, including the legate Arnaud-Amaury, now bishop of Narbonne, were abusing their spiritual authority to amass material power and wealth. Innocent wrote to his legates: 'You have stretched out your greedy hands towards lands which no taint of heresy ever sullied.'

Despite the pope's change of heart, the bishops of Toulouse and Carcassonne continued to preach the Crusade against the Cathars in the territory of the French king. This went against Pedro's interests. Fresh from his triumph in Spain, Pedro was looking for ways of diminishing Montfort's influence over the conquered towns and cities, much preferring the vassals he was used to – Toulouse and Trencavel – to the belligerent, self-righteous zealot from the north. Partly in response to his diplomacy, Raymond VI and his son, Raymond the Younger, both reaffirmed their surface commitment to the Catholic church, idly promising once more to rid their lands of 'heresy'. Even Raymond-Roger of Foix was brought on side.

Pedro looked further afield and attempted to persuade King Philippe-Auguste of France to give him permission to marry his daughter. In Rome, however, Marie of Montpellier had been successful. Pope Innocent promised Marie that her marriage with Pedro would not be dissolved and commanded Pedro to live 'as a good spouse'. No sooner was this news made public than Marie fell ill. In writing his report, Marie's physician asked for the assistance of the pope's personal doctor. They affirmed: 'Poison helped to end her days.'

The date was 19 April 1213. No other evidence was advanced and Marie of Montpellier was buried in Rome. Her reluctant husband only outlived her for a matter of months.

⚏ CHAPTER 33 ⚏

The Battle of Muret

*I*n the spring of 1213, Pope Innocent III decided, after all, that he had no military choice but Montfort, no spiritual choice but Arnaud-Amaury. He bowed to the pressure of their letters and embassies and, on 21 May 1213, Innocent wrote to Pedro of Aragon to confirm that he had no faith in the new vows of Toulouse. He asked Pedro to establish a durable ceasefire with Montfort. At the same time, Innocent wrote to Montfort, commanding him to respect his status as a feudal vassal of Aragon. Neither took any notice.

In July 1213, Montfort officially broke off all feudal obligations towards the house of Aragon. The combat in Languedoc came down to a simple equation: on the one hand the Crusader army led by Montfort, on the other the houses of Aragon, Toulouse and Foix, the remnants of Trencavel and other lesser nobility of the *langue d'oc*. The decisive battle took place at Muret, 15 kilometres southwest of Toulouse.

The town of Muret occupied an island in the Garonne, at the point where it was joined by its tributary, the Louge. It was at the limit of land held by the count of Comminges, an independent enclave. Pedro got there first and chose to set up camp on a gentle rise in the land about 1,500 metres west of the confluence of the two rivers. Foulques of Toulouse wrote to the king to advise him to surrender or withdraw, but Pedro didn't deign to answer.

Montfort made all possible haste to assemble his own army. His wife, Alix, went to Carcassonne to gather support. On 10 September 1213, Montfort marched from Fanjeaux at the head of a column of 1,000 knights plus at least seven bishops, including Arnaud-Amaury. The last night at Fanjeaux, Alix dreamt she saw her husband with his arms covered in blood. He paid no attention, asking her: 'Do you think I believe in dreams and auguries like some Spaniard?'

Nevertheless, he stopped en route to nurture his own superstitions. At the Cistercian abbey of Boulbonne he prayed for God's assistance. One of the clerics counselled prudence in battle. Montfort showed the cleric an intercepted letter, written by the philandering Pedro to a noble lady of Toulouse, and replied: 'I have no fear of a king who comes forth for a courtesan in the affairs of God.' But he took the precaution of drafting a will and signing it with his seal to be kept by the abbey.

The same day, 10 September, the forces of the counts of Toulouse, Comminges and Foix and the Toulouse militia, led by the city consuls, entered Pedro's camp on the gentle hill. On the evening of the next day, Montfort's army entered Muret from the east, tramping across a wooden bridge that spanned the Garonne.

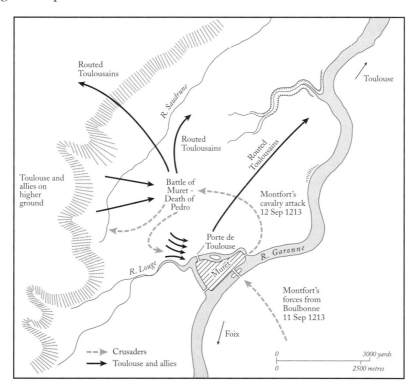

The siege at Muret

Debate ensued in either camp. Raymond VI advised the building of defences – palisades and ditches – to protect their position and decimate the enemy charge. He was opposed by his more ardent allies who favoured 'chivalrous stratagems' – in other words, all-out attack. In Montfort's camp, there was concern that the force at their disposal was far too small. The clerics offered to go barefoot to Pedro and negotiate a withdrawal. Montfort would have none of it. Even when, on the morning of battle, his belt broke and he was knocked on the head by his mount, he refused to countenance delay.

Montfort led out three troops of cavalry, inviting attack, then hung back in the third group himself. Pedro had also advanced three bodies of horsemen, positioning himself in the second corps and exchanging armour with one of his men. He gave the order for one group to charge and the Crusaders retreated on to the flat ground, removing the advantage of height from Pedro's forces. All at once the Crusaders turned and faced the attack in a devastating clash of arms. As the line of Crusader horses began to give ground, Montfort launched his second group, drawing Pedro's own corps into the combat. The soldier who was wearing Pedro's armour was brought down. To prevent his troops from becoming discouraged, Pedro called out to his men not to worry, that he was safe, that the other was an impostor. The king of Aragon was immediately and fatally struck down by a Crusader lance.

Leaderless and appalled, the alliance of Toulouse gave ground on all sides. The battle swiftly became a rout when many of the mounted men fled. The habit of victory was not theirs; they were accustomed to defeat and flight. The Crusader cavalry raced into the camp of the southern alliance with catastrophic results for the defenders. Only the Toulouse militia fought on with any purpose, making their way into the *castrum* of Muret itself, before themselves being caught in a pincer movement as the Crusader cavalry returned to the city from two sides. Many of them threw themselves in the Garonne and drowned. Others escaped northeast towards Toulouse. One chronicler wrote: 'There was barely a house in Toulouse that hadn't a death to mourn.'

At the end of the battle, Pedro's corpse was discovered naked on the field. Montfort showed respect to his fallen adversary by handing over his body to the Knights Hospitaller of Toulouse. The clerics condemned Pedro roundly: 'It is deeply to be deplored that such a noble and powerful lord should ally himself with the enemies of Christ and fight the allies of Christ and of the Holy Church.'

For some reason, Montfort didn't press home his advantage. Raymond VI and his son fled to Toulouse, but Montfort decided not to follow them and attack the *ville rose* itself. Perhaps he was concerned that he had overreached himself in killing Pedro, a reigning Catholic monarch, sworn vassal of Pope Innocent III. Perhaps he judged that he wouldn't be lucky twice in a row with limited resources. Perhaps he didn't like the look of the weather – the campaign season of 1213 was, after all, virtually over.

Raymond decided that his only option now was to make his peace with the pope. For this, he judged that he would have to visit Rome in person. Meanwhile, in Languedoc, the dreadful news travelled from town to town and from town to village, each a day's mournful march apart. There would be no great alliance to repel the Crusaders. Pedro was dead.

The patriotic author of the *Canso*, writing as the events unfolded, said: 'Word is spreading already, a dark rumour of disaster…What a blow fell there, what a fatality, what awful agony when the king of Aragon lay bleeding on the grass. What a loss, the death of so many knights. Shame on Christendom to have allowed it.'

⛋ CHAPTER 34 ⛋

The *Canso* of *Anònim*

hy anonymous? Because no one knows who wrote 70 per cent of *La Canso de la Crosada*. Guilhèm of Tudèla composed the first 3,000-odd lines in his rather workaday verse, bringing the story forward to the preparations for the Battle of Muret in July 1213. Then he stopped. His master, Baldwin of Toulouse, the traitorous younger brother of Raymond VI, was hanged in 1214, nearly a year later. Perhaps Guilhèm was killed or imprisoned. Perhaps, in the end, the task sickened him.

When the text of the *Canso* was rediscovered and published in 1837, the search for the 'second' – more gifted – author began. Quickly, researchers realised that whoever it was must have been present at a number of key events – historic events, in fact.

On 19 April 1213, Pope Innocent III summoned the Fourth Council of the Lateran in Rome. While the war ground on in Languedoc, perhaps 1,500

The Lateran Palace was given to the Bishop of Rome by Constantine I. It is shown here in an 18th-century engraving.

clerics, noblemen and ambassadors met in November 1215. They spent some time reaffirming the beliefs of the Catholic church, then moved on to those who dared to disagree with its doctrines:

We condemn, therefore, and reprobate the book or tract which Abbott Joachim published against Master Peter Lombard concerning the unity or essence of the Trinity, calling him heretical and insane…We excommunicate and anathematise every heresy that raises against the holy, Orthodox and Catholic faith…condemning all heretics under whatever names they may be known, for while they have different faces they are nevertheless bound to each other by their tails…Those condemned, being handed over to the secular rulers of their bailiffs, let them be abandoned, to be punished with due justice…As to the property of the condemned…let it be confiscated…We decree that those who give credence to the teachings of the heretics, as well as those who receive, defend and patronise them, are excommunicated.

Innocent knew that a good deal of the success of the 'heretics' could be attributed to the corruption and opulence – or possibly indifference – of its own clergy: 'By an irrefragable decree we ordain that prelates make a prudent and earnest effort to correct the excesses and reform the morals of their subjects, especially of the clergy, lest their blood be demanded at their hands.'

This passage continues by asserting that the representatives of the Catholic church were above the law: 'But that they may perform unhindered the duty of correction and reform, we decree that no custom or appeal shall stand in the way of their efforts.'

Raymond VI of Toulouse and his son, Raymond the Younger, the future Raymond VII, were present at the council with Raymond-Roger of Foix. They argued against the confiscation of their territories. Foulques, the Catholic bishop of Toulouse, and a Spanish evangelist named Domingo de Guzmán unsurprisingly argued in favour. So did Simon of Montfort's brother Guy. *Anònim* was there too. But who was he?

Of course, *Anònim* must have been a *trobador*. One suggestion was a poet from Toulouse called Guillaume Anelier, the author of the *Song of the War of Navarre*, which closely mirrors the structure of the *Canso*. Others put forward a woman poet from Quercy called Dormonde or a Toulousain lawyer, Bernard d'Ulmo, who appears in the *Canso* as '*maître* Bernard'. Much more convincing was the case made for Gui, a *trobador* from Cavaillon in Provence who took part in the resistance alongside Raymond the Younger and was present at the Lateran Council and other key events.

Anònim was not a Cathar. His vivid *Canso* is no more sympathetic to the 'heretics' than Tudèla's and he piously invokes Jesus, the Holy Spirit and the Virgin Mary. But, unlike Guilhèm, an adoptive son of Languedoc, *Anònim* was a patriot, a native of the Midi. For *Anònim*, the Crusaders were foreign invaders, bent on destroying *paratge* – including the enhanced role of women.

Medieval Catholic law followed Roman law in limiting the rights of women, whereas in Languedoc a daughter had the same rights of inheritance as her brothers. The average age of marriage was eighteen years old and the dowry given by the bride's family remained her own to invest or dilapidate as she saw fit, without requiring the permission of her husband. The dowry – always the most important clause of any 12th-century marriage contract – was generally seen as an advance payment, in full, of the fortune liable to be inherited on the death of the bride's parents. Many young women benefitted far in advance of their brothers. If any daughters remained unmarried on the death of their parents, their parents' wills often specified that their sons should take on the responsibility of providing their sisters with a suitable dowry.

The women of Languedoc could also own other property not acquired by dowry or inheritance, including land, both privately and within the pyramid of feudal responsibility. She could will her property as she saw fit and had full rights to go into business, borrow and lend, offer herself as a guarantor or pursue defaulters in the courts – and be pursued herself.

In some respects, there was no advantage to being a woman of Toulouse. Just as in Rome 1,000 years earlier, women were excluded from the civil service. According to the laws of the city, an adulterous wife might be shaved, whipped and confined in a nunnery for as long as her husband desired it. (A man caught in similar circumstances was subject to no punishment whatsoever.) On the other hand, the laws of the ville rose removed from the cuckolded husband the right to kill his wife if he caught her in the act…unless she and her partner refused to obey his commands to desist.

All of this meant that the noble domains of the southwest were splintered between male and female children. In the 12th century, barely any towns of the plains could boast a single *seigneur* as authority was divided between multiple *co-seigneurs* and *co-seigneuresses*. This tradition created a natural set of checks and balances in terms of the relationships of power between regions and towns, but it also often meant government by committee. The men of Languedoc were quite aware of the practices of other regions and they often complained at the dispersal of hard-won family wealth. But it was a key element of the particular society extolled by *Anònim*.

In the *Canso*, *paratge* is associated with words like generosity of spirit and heart, right and truth, loyalty and personal merit. It is contrasted with pride, bad faith, deceit and cunning. Montfort's barbaric strategy of 'pacification' is portrayed, by *Anònim*, as a sequence of war crimes. Resistance is extolled and, when *Anònim* tells the story of the death of Pedro of Aragon at Muret, he laments the end of the coalition to save the 'people of our language' from the invaders: 'Know this for truth, in this moment all humankind was diminished, *paratge* was killed and exiled and all Christianity brought low and shamed.'

It would be five long years more before *Anònim* could write his verses of vengeance, alongside Raymond the Younger at the siege of Toulouse.

☒ CHAPTER 35 ☒

Dominic

espite the death of Pedro of Aragon, despite the mutilations, retributions and attrition, Languedoc remained unsubdued. The *Bons Chrétiens* continued their popular ministry. From the Catholics, a new strategy began to take form.

The Catholic Inquisition was founded at the beginning of the 13th century for the purpose of exterminating the Cathars and other 'heretics'. The first steps towards its murderous bureaucracy were taken by Pope Innocent III at the Fourth Council of the Lateran in Rome in November 1215. At the council, he had discussions with two men who were intimately acquainted with the success of the Cathars – Foulques, the Catholic bishop of Toulouse and the Spanish monk Domingo de Guzmán.

Guzmán was born, around 1170, into an old Castilian Spanish family. After studies of philosophy and theology, he entered the church and, around 1203, was sent on a mission to Denmark. The journey took him through Languedoc, where he discovered the ubiquity of the *Bons Chrétiens*. On his return journey, he visited Cîteaux and Rome before settling in southwest France. He set himself the task of converting the population to the church of Rome.

Guzmán had an advantage over many Catholic clergy of the time in that he lived a life similar in poverty and piety to his Cathar opponents. Some say this was a strategy he developed in an attempt to match their exemplary conduct. As Montfort's war raged about him, with his ascetic appearance he gained the respect of the Cathar priests he met. He walked from village to town on his bare and bloody feet and engaged the *Bons Chrétiens* in debates, some of which lasted a week or more. But his successes were very limited. So he developed a new strategy and he and a fellow brother founded a convent at Prouille, below the Cathar hill town of Fanjeaux, in about 1206.

Originally from Marseille, the Cistercian Foulques was an important supporter of the Crusade and had founded the Toulouse militia, the *Conférerie Blanche*. He gave Guzmán permission to use the church at Prouille but financial support was poor and the buildings were dilapidated. Progress was slow. A few years later, in 1211, Foulques donated from his own pocket the revenues due to him from Prouille in order to support Guzmán's work. The convent also received donations from members of Montfort's Crusade, the largest reputedly coming from Montfort himself.

Guzmán's strategy of creating a Catholic convent was a good one. The Cathar priesthood was open to women – although there is no record of any woman becoming a deacon or bishop – and Cathar communities of retreat existed throughout the region. Guzmán was aware that there were very few competing Catholic convents and they hoped – perhaps naïvely – that Prouille could become a haven for the women he sought to convert from Catharism.

Despite the failures, at the Lateran in 1215, Guzmán's eminence as an evangelist led Pope Innocent III to give official approval to the foundation of his monastic order. They are sometimes known as the Order of Preachers or – due to the colour of the cowl they wore – the Black Friars. More often they are named after Domingo de Guzmán himself – the Dominicans.

The following year, Innocent died in Perugia. He succumbed to repeated bouts of fever, possibly brought on by malaria. His corpse was displayed in a church and, the following day, stripped of its fine vestments by thieves. It began visibly to rot in the close summer heat before being interred. (In 1890, the remains were transferred to the Lateran in Rome.)

Innocent was followed by Pope Honorius III, a Roman nobleman, who confirmed the establishment of several new orders of monks, including the Dominicans in 1216 and, later, the Franciscans. The future St Dominic lived long enough to see the Crusade against the Cathars falter and begin to stall.

Guzmán died in 1221 and was canonised in 1234. Swiftly, a set of stories – a hagiography – grew up around his career as an evangelist. The location of the convent at Prouille, it seems, was indicated by a shaft of divine light that he perceived while meditating the intransigence of the 'heretics' on the walls of Fanjeaux. Another story, told many times by artists, poets and theologians, tells the legend of the holy books and the ordeal by fire. In the course of a debate with some 'heretic' theologians, a Cathar New Testament and Dominic's own Bible were placed in a fire. The Cathar book was consumed whilst Domingo's Bible leapt from the flames. This legend was

Pedro Berruguete's 15th-century portrayal of Domingo and the burning books.

supposed to show that Domingo's preaching was accompanied by the grace and protection of God. Of course, had such a scene ever taken place, the Cathars would have laughed aloud at the idea that God's grace could be tested by burning a book – a material artefact from this base Earth, created by the Devil himself for the purposes of entrapment and deceit.

Despite the hagiography, Guzmán was never an inquisitor. The order he founded was not given the task of investigating the sources and seats of heresy until twelve years after his death. Once it had taken on the role, it became convenient for Catholic historians to suggest that the work had begun at Prouille in 1206. (Alongside the Black Monks, the Cistercians in their white cowls also performed the ignoble office.)

It is said that Guzmán's real stroke of genius was in sending his brother monks to the great centres of theological debate in Paris and Bologna, the better to arm them in their discussions with 'heretic' preachers and believers, yet conversions were few. Despite his theological and philosophical training, Guzmán and his closest companions were clearly out of their depth in religious debate and had no understanding of the status of 'donas e tozas e mulhers' – 'ladies and girls and women' – in Languedoc society. One of his companions rudely commanded Esclarmonde, the sister of the count of Foix no less, to keep silent and not interrupt the men in their religious debate. It is unlikely that she was tempted to embrace this boorish man's faith.

Guzmán himself is known to have used physical violence on those he tried to convert and his hectoring, exasperated style failed to conceal the Catholic church's underlying territorial ambition:

*F*or many years I have spoken to you with gentle words, preaching, begging, weeping. But, as the proverb says in my country, 'where fine words fail, clubs prevail'. So we will call up against you the princes and the prelates. They will gather nations and kingdoms together against your country. Many will perish by the sword, towers will be thrown down, walls demolished and ruined and – what misery! – you will all be reduced to slavery.

⛩ CHAPTER 36 ⛩

The Death of Montfort

etween the fall of Carcassonne in 1209 and 1215, Montfort's victories were so conclusive that the prince of France, the future Louis VIII, came to Languedoc, more as a pilgrim than as a Crusader. He was kept well away from any live fighting. Once his forty days were up, he made haste to return north to the court of his father, Philippe-Auguste.

The following year, 1216, Raymond VI of Toulouse and his son, Raymond the Younger, were in France, though not necessarily in their capital. With their allies in Languedoc and Provence, they were hatching a plan to lead a pincer attack on Montfort. In response, Montfort sent a pre-emptive force to attack Raymond the Younger in the town of Beaucaire, Raymond's birthplace near Avignon, where Toulouse had many allies.

Montfort's expedition established a siege but couldn't cut off the supplies of food and arms from the river Rhône and had to abandon it. In fact, the Toulouse forces were so well stocked that they turned the tables. Montfort's army became besieged in its turn and had to sue for surrender. Eventually this was granted and Raymond the Younger, the future Raymond VII, had scored his first important victory. It probably marked the beginning of the end for Montfort.

Beaucaire had shown that Toulouse had many allies still and that Montfort's forces were stretched. Wherever he took a town or stronghold by force, he was obliged to garrison it, for fear of losing it as soon as his back was turned. In September 1216, his troops, led by his brother Guy, pillaged the *ville rose*, alienating the people and storing up more resentment. It was the act, perhaps, of a man who understood that the climate of fear and repression that he had so carefully and barbarically nurtured had been dispelled. Although in the spring of the following year Montfort accepted the surrender of Peyrepertuse, previously believed impregnable, his army was difficult to manage, renewed as it was only periodically by new Crusaders.

On the morning of 13 September 1217, Raymond VI returned to Toulouse. He was assisted by the pockets of resistance that had spontaneously sprung up following Guy of Montfort's pillaging. The population turned on the northerners and their collaborators in the city and many had to seek refuge in the cathedrals and abbeys. Raymond immediately gave orders for the city's fortifications to be restored and virtually the whole population joined in the effort. He re-established the city's twenty-four consuls, representatives of the people that Montfort had abolished. Reinforcements flooded into the city from all around, dispossessed knights and *seigneurs* from Cabardès, Minervois, Corbières, Carcassès, Lauragais and the Pyrenees.

Montfort wrote to the Catholic archbishop of Auch and the new pope, Honorius III, for assistance. In October, he pitched camp about 15 kilometres southeast of Toulouse and was joined by the army of his brother Guy. They advanced to the gates of the city but reinforcements continued on the side of Toulouse. Raymond-Roger, count of Foix, soon arrived, fighting his way past the troops of Montfort's son Amaury.

As summer came to an end, the two sides skirmished over river access, bridges and roads, but no weakness in the city's defences could be found. Montfort decided – once more – that he would have to resort to a siege. But the siege season was already more or less over. The status quo persisted throughout the winter. Only with the return of good weather at Easter 1218 did the fighting resume.

Perhaps aware that hot summer sun would make things difficult for the besieged forces of Toulouse, the defenders organised successful sorties to pick off members of the Crusader army. At the beginning of May, Montfort sent his two most valuable and trusted collaborators – his wife, Alix, and Foulques, bishop of Toulouse – to France in search of reinforcements with thirty of his best knights. Thus depleted, Montfort's forces were repulsed by the troops of Foix from the suburb of Saint-Cyprien to the west of the city. Then, in a stroke of good fortune for Montfort, three days of torrential rain made the river Garonne burst its banks. Saint-Cyprien was abandoned by its defenders. As the waters fell, Montfort marched in.

The habit of defeat was deeply ingrained in Raymond VI of Toulouse. In his son's absence, this relatively minor setback seems to have prompted him to draw up a new will, bequeathing – among other things – the revenues from his tenant farmers to the Knights Hospitaller and the Knights Templar of the city.

On 2 June, the first major Crusader attack broke like a wave on the defences – the ditches and palisades held. The Crusaders began assembling their siege engines, including a huge *chatte* – a shelter on wheels designed to protect the attackers from attack from the walls. Then, on 7 June, the bells of the city rang out joyfully to announce the arrival of Raymond the Younger, the twenty-one-year-old future Raymond VII, with a troop of knights from Provence.

In any case, inside the city, the entire population had been mobilised. The first line of defence – defensive siege weapons installed behind the walls – was fantastically successful, driving back the attacks and smashing the enormous *chatte* to smithereens. The Crusaders couldn't get within fighting range of the fortifications. In mid-June, Montfort gathered his commanders together to tell them, with his customary recklessness, that he wanted the city razed to the ground within one month. While his lieutenants and soldiers were beginning to doubt Montfort's ability to continue to triumph over irrational odds, Simon himself nourished visions of wiping the *ville rose* entirely from the map, banishing 'heretics' and their protectors for ever.

The next day, Monday, 25 June 1218, a Toulousain sortie engaged the troops of Guy of Montfort at a place called Le Pré Montoulieu, just outside the city walls. Simon threw himself into the skirmish. Guy took an arrow from a crossbow in the side and Simon ran to help him. At the same moment, a stone thrown by a mangonel operated by a team of '*donas e tozas e mulhers*' – 'ladies and girls and women' – came soaring over the fortifications and struck him down. He was dead. *Anònim*, the anonymous author of the second part of *La Canso de la Crosada* was there:

> *E venc tot dreit la peira lai on era mestiers*
> *E ferric si lo comté sobre l'elm qu'es d'acres,*
> *Que'ls olhs e las cervelas e'ls caichals estremiers,*
> *E'l front et las maichelas li partic a cartiers.*
> *E'l coms cazec en terra mostrz e sagnens e niers…*
> *E ar Paratges alumpna es er oimais sobrers.*

> And the stone came straight where it was needed
> And clouted the count on his helmet made of steel,

So his eyes and his brains and his back teeth
And his forehead and his jaw burst into pieces.
And he fell dead on the ground, bloody and black…
Paratge shone forth once more in everlasting triumph.

The judgement was premature. Montfort was given a memorial service in Sant-Nasari in the Cité of Carcassonne and *Anònim* concluded, with bitter sarcasm:

The epitaph says, for those who can read, that he was a saint and a martyr who will live again…wearing a crown, resplendent in Heaven…But I think that if, by killing and shedding blood, condemning souls and provoking murders, believing bad counsel and lighting pyres, destroying our lords and banishing *paratge*, arrogantly stealing our lands, spreading evil and shaming good, massacring mothers and cutting their children's throats – if this is a good way of honouring Jesus Christ, then yes, Montfort is indeed crowned and resplendent in Heaven.

⛊ CHAPTER 37 ⛊

Undefeated

ews of Montfort's death on 25 June 1218 spread rapidly throughout Toulouse and 'joy was unrestrained'. Raymond the Younger, just twenty-one years old but a veteran of exile and war, slipped out of the besieged city to prepare the defences elsewhere, but was back at his father's side by 1 July.

Amaury of Montfort was twenty years old. As quickly as it could be arranged, Amaury was invested with all his father's possessions – the conquests of the Crusade against the Cathars from Béziers and Carcassonne onwards – and was confirmed a vassal of the French king. Then he faced, for the first time, the kind of perpetual interruption that dogged his father's campaign.

A large body of his Crusader army was preparing to return north at the end of their forty days' service. Despite this, Amaury ordered another attack on Toulouse. It is unlikely the hearts of his men were in it and it quickly failed. There would be no other. The siege was over. All that remained was for the Crusaders to burn their camp and siege engines and fall back to Carcassonne.

Amaury discussed his father's inheritance with his brother, Simon the Younger. Between them, they decided to split their father's estate. Simon the Younger walked away with the paper titles to property and lordship in Leicester.

Amaury had his father's body sewn up in an ox skin and boiled and took what appeared to be the lion's share – the extraordinary possessions Montfort had wrested from the houses of Trencavel, Toulouse and Aragon. But the talisman didn't help him to live up to his father's reputation, or his new status as count of Toulouse and *de facto* leader of the Crusade. He was unable to reproduce his father's extraordinary ability to be in the right place at the right time. Raymond the Younger recaptured city after city, town after town.

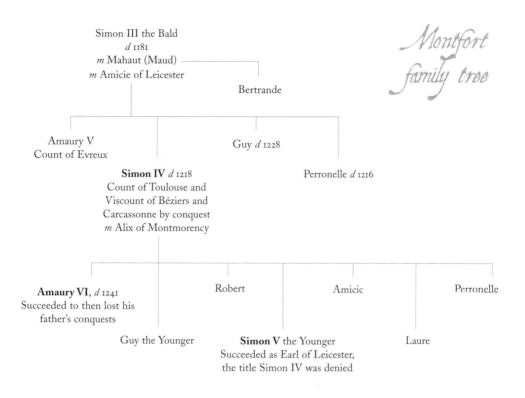

Simon III the Bald
d 1181
m Mahaut (Maud)
m Amicie of Leicester

Montfort family tree

Bertrande

Amaury V
Count of Evreux

Guy *d* 1228

Simon IV *d* 1218
Count of Toulouse and
Viscount of Béziers and
Carcassonne by conquest
m Alix of Montmorency

Perronelle *d* 1216

Amaury VI, *d* 1241
Succeeded to then lost his
father's conquests

Robert

Amicic

Perronelle

Guy the Younger

Simon V the Younger
Succeeded as Earl of Leicester,
the title Simon IV was denied

Laure

The failed siege of Toulouse was not just the end of Simon of Montfort; it was an opportunity for the throne of France. In 1219, Louis, prince of France, once more came south, this time not as a pilgrim but as a true Crusader, with an army of something between 25,000 and 100,000 men. (It's hard to judge from the partial historical commentaries.)

Was Louis motivated by the repeated entreaties from Pope Honorius III in the Vatican? Was it dawning on him that the time was ripe for the French monarchy finally to conquer the independence of the *Miègjorn* – the Midi?

The test of the new axis Montfort-France came at Marmande in June 1219. The town surrendered to the combined forces in return for the lives of the population being spared. This was agreed. The gates were opened and the man who would become Louis VIII of France watched as his soldiers massacred 5,000 unarmed citizens, men, women, children, the infirm and the aged.

The combined forces of France and Amaury's Crusaders left Marmande and marched on Toulouse. Louis was clearly as much of a barbarian as Amaury's father, but he did not have Montfort's devastating persistence. Raymond the Younger's defences were too discouraging and the siege was abandoned on 1 August. Louis returned north, leaving behind a corps of 200 French knights for one year only.

A new phase in the Crusade against the Cathars had begun. The Crusade led by the barons of the north was, effectively, over. Despite the fact that Amaury had proved himself his father's equal in war crimes, he was incapable of imitating his father's strategic success. Between 1220 and 1226, Languedoc and the 'people of our language' rose up in support of their independence.

In 1220, two years after Montfort's death, Raymond the Younger of Toulouse, Raymond VI's son, retook the town of Lavaur and murdered every member of its garrison. At the siege of Castelnaudary in 1220, Amaury's brother Guy was killed while, safe within the walls, lived Gaucelm, the Cathar bishop of Toulouse, his deputy, Guilhabert of Castres, and the future Cathar bishop of Razès, Raymond Agulher. (Before becoming bishop, a Cathar *parfait* would progress through two lower ranks, *filius minor* and *filius major* – lesser and greater son. Guilhabert was Gaucelm's *filius major*.)

For Amaury, Castelnaudary was just one of a sequence of defeats. Things didn't improve for Montfort's inheritor when, in 1222, Raymond VI died on his way to pray in one of the Catholic churches of Toulouse.

Raymond was struck dumb by a sudden illness in the street. He collapsed to the ground and struggled to explain by gesture that he wished to reconcile himself to the Catholic church. He was brought the cape of a Knight Hospitaller of St John – the order to whom he had willed his tenant farms before the siege of Toulouse – and kissed the cross embroidered upon it. Then he expired. In accordance with his will, his body was taken for burial by the Hospitallers but, excommunicated by the Catholic church, hallowed ground was denied him. His coffin was stored in a shed in the Hospitallers' courtyard for many years while his son attempted to have the judgment overturned. Then rats gnawed their way in and scattered his bones.

Raymond the Younger became Count Raymond VII of Toulouse, surely strengthening the resolve of the *Miègjorn*. The following year, Philippe-Auguste of France died, succeeded by Louis VIII. Despite his two previous ventures south, Louis wasn't interested in the conflict in Languedoc at this point. By 1224 Amaury's position was desperate. On 14 January, he met with the leaders of the southern alliance on the banks of the river Aude, at the foot of the ramparts of Carcassonne, to sign the document of surrender. Then he took the road north, carrying with him the remains of his father sewn into the skin of an ox.

☲ CHAPTER 38 ☲

The Possibility of Peace

*I*n 1224, when Amaury of Montfort left Languedoc, Raymond VII of Toulouse, previously known as Raymond the Younger, was twenty-seven years old. His ally Count Roger-Bernard II of Foix was perhaps two years older. Raymond Trencavel, the son of Raymond-Roger Trencavel and Agnès of Montpellier, was just sixteen.

Between them, the counts of Toulouse and Foix, two icons of southern independence, worked to restore the Trencavel lands to their heir. At last, young Raymond Trencavel went back to Carcassonne to live. For a few short years, peace appeared possible. The Cathar bishop of Carcassonne, Pierre Isarn, made Cabaret the seat of his diocese and was joined by many *parfaits* and believers, including dispossessed knights like Olivier of Termes. Throughout Languedoc, the *Bons Chrétiens* resumed their preaching, comforting and consoling.

Raymond VII sent embassies to Pope Honorius in Rome, submitting to the Catholic church's will, at least on paper. The three young lords of Languedoc met with the archbishop of Narbonne, Arnaud-Amaury, the 'worst of the Cistercians', and repeated their devotion to his church. But they wanted changes in the settlement put in place by Amaury of Montfort that made the lands of the southwest vassals of the French king – they demanded the return of the feudal allegiances from prior to the Barons' Crusade against the Cathars. In return, they promised to expel the mercenaries and the 'heretics' from their lands.

Arnaud-Amaury died at Fontfroide in September 1225. Diplomatic machinations continued behind the scenes for months. A new council was summoned and Raymond VII was invited to repeat his vow to rid his lands of 'heresy'. He did so, fulsomely. The council then demanded that he renounce all title to the domains of Toulouse, his dynastic home, in his own name and those of his descendants. It was clear to Raymond that diplomacy had failed. For the Catholics and the French, in the end, only territorial conquest counted – the extirpation of 'heresy' was a pretext.

Raymond's father, Raymond VI, would have tried to find a way of procrastinating, of delaying the deadline. Raymond VII acted more decisively and firmly declined the poisoned pill. He was condemned as 'unreconciled'. The council called on Louis VIII of France to lead a new

An image of Louis VIII from the mid-14th century

Crusade. In January 1226, Louis agreed and Raymond VII was excommunicated, removing all his legal rights of ownership to his property and lands. On 17 May 1226, the beginning of the campaigning season for another dreadful year, a new *Ost gran* assembled. Alongside the king of France were Amaury of Montfort, his uncle Guy of Montfort and Bouchard of Marly, another grizzled veteran of the Barons' Crusade who had negotiated the surrender of Cabaret in the spring of 1211.

No one in Languedoc wanted war. In the southwest, there was terror and a stampede of devotion. The new archbishop of Narbonne, Pierre Amiel, received guarantees of commitment to the Catholic church from numerous towns and villages, as did many other Catholic prelates. But when the Host reached Avignon, Louis found that Raymond had managed to galvanise the courage of the people – the gates were shut against the Crusaders. Louis established a siege of the town on 6 June 1226 which would not end until 12 September. The city endured more than three months of deprivation, combat and disease before, exhausted, it surrendered.

Also in September, Toulouse and Foix renewed their southern alliance with a new treaty. Louis quickly set up a seneschal – a kind of royal governor – in Avignon, Beaucaire and Nîmes. Carcassonne submitted to the royal will and a seneschal was appointed for the Cité too. Young Raymond Trencavel was absent in safety. Perhaps unaware that Louis VIII was already dangerously ill, in October, Amaury of Montfort signed away his rights to Pamiers, in the foothills of the Pyrenees, to the French king,

Louis left the Pyrenees and went back down to the plains of Lauragais, accepting tributes from Castelnaudary and Lavaur. In Albi, he paused to raise the pension allotted to Agnès of Montpellier, Raymond Trencavel's mother, the widow of Raymond-Roger Trencavel. Then he left behind in Languedoc an army under the command of Imbert of Beaujeu. Imbert's forces arrested the Cathar bishop Pierre Isarn on the road to Toulouse and handed him over to Pierre Amiel. Amiel showed himself a 'worthy' successor to Arnaud-Amaury by promptly ordering him burnt at the stake.

The royal procession moved north and the king's condition worsened. The column crossed the volcanic mountains of the Puy-de-Dôme before stopping to allow Louis VIII to expire a few kilometres north of Clermont-Ferrand on 8 November 1226 at Montpensier. Again there was, perhaps, an opportunity for peace.

The 'heretic' Cathar church still had deep roots. At the start of the Crusade in 1209, there were three Cathar bishops: Toulouse, Carcassonne and Albi. In 1226, after perhaps 1,500 *parfaits* had been executed, most of them burnt alive, the Cathar church was in good enough health to create a fourth bishop at Razès. Furthermore, Louis' heir, Louis IX of France, was just twelve years old. Louis' mother, Blanche of Castile, was made regent and many French aristocrats took advantage of the delayed succession to rebel and Blanche was obliged to put all her energy into combating this threat. There was even an attempt to kidnap young Louis. Languedoc was relegated to the background.

Raymond Trencavel and the count of Foix re-established rule over Limoux, south of Carcassonne on the river Aude, in company with at least forty *faydits*, including Pierre-Roger of Mirepoix. In the winter of 1226–7, Raymond VII captured Auterive, south of Toulouse on the river Ariège, from its French garrison. Raymond reinforced the defences at Labécède and, in the summer, as he expected, the town was besieged by Imbert of Beaujeu. Outnumbered, the armed defenders fled and Imbert also showed himself a 'worthy' successor to Montfort's Crusade by murdering the entire population, including a large number of *parfaits*. Combats around Limoux and, above all, Cabaret put a large number of Cathar *Bons Chrétiens* in danger, so they were smuggled away by *faydits*.

Imbert then besieged Lagrave and rampaged across the region of Cordes. In the meantime, Guilhabert of Castres, a Cathar priest of exemplary reputation, established a home in Saint-Paul-Cap-de-Joux, east of Toulouse near Lavaur. He was a tireless preacher, capable – like many of his kind – of walking almost superhuman distances, converting and consoling his people. There are records of his preaching in several hundred different locations in Languedoc, including many close escapes from capture. In Saint-Paul at this time he lived openly and received visits from many members of the Cathar church.

In Rome in 1227, there were changes too. Pope Honorius III was dead, replaced by Gregory IX. Gregory's name was Ugolino di Conti and he was the nephew of Innocent III, who launched the Crusade against the Cathars. He – like his uncle – was determined that the Catholic church should assert and reassert its primacy in temporal affairs as well as spiritual affairs. For Gregory, like Innocent, it was not enough that salvation should only be attainable through the Catholic church – kings, princes and governments should bend to the pope's will as well. But he was, in addition, a politician. He devised and put forward a plan that might ensure peace between the monarchy of France and the house of Toulouse.

⚏ CHAPTER 39 ⚏
The Humiliation of Raymond VII

*P*ope Gregory IX's idea was to seal a new treaty between France and Toulouse with the marriage of Jeanne, the daughter of Raymond VII and Sanchia of Aragon, daughter of the late King Pedro, to one of young Louis IX's brothers. Louis's mother, Blanche of Castile, agreed with Gregory's plan and encouraged it. She was fully aware of the cost of the war in the south. What was more, her allegiances were divided. She was such a close relative of Raymond of Toulouse that the pope had to order a derogation of the rules of consanguinity so that the marriage between her son and Raymond's daughter could be entertained.

At the same time, in Languedoc, like Simon and then Amaury of Montfort before him, Imbert of Beaujeu had the greatest difficulty in juggling the periodic arrival and departure of his troops of forty-day Crusaders. In the summer of 1228, he welcomed troops raised by the bishop of Auch and led them in a devastating attack on the lands around Toulouse, ripping the vines out of the ground and destroying all the food crops. He then advanced up the valley of the Ariège to within sight of the château of Foix.

As the debilitating war continued, Raymond VII surely had to favour the pope's plan. He was, it seemed, being offered the treaty he had expected to sign at the previous council, before being presented with the poisoned pill of destitution. Several *châteaux* of the southwest jumped the gun and surrendered or professed allegiance to the king of France. Raymond appointed a negotiator to debate the treaty with Blanche of Castile's representative. By December, because of the devastation of its crops by Imbert's army, the city of Toulouse was starving. A meeting was organised in Meaux in Champagne and the treaty was finally signed in Paris on 12 April 1229. (Some history books call it the Treaty of Meaux, some the Treaty of Paris.)

Once again, Raymond found that he had been led up the garden path. The treaty placed on the table was the same capitulation he had previously refused. Of the thirty-two articles in the treaty, thirty-one listed the obligations of Toulouse. He was to drive out 'heresy', keep the peace, remove the *routiers* – mercenaries – and sack any 'heretics' or Jews who held public office. Enormous sums in reparations were required to be paid to the Catholic church, including special payments to the abbeys of, among others, Cîteaux and Clairvaux. In articles 5 and 6, Raymond was obliged to admit the primacy of the Catholic authorities in the repression of 'heresy'. He was to 'take the cross' and spend at least five years crusading in the Holy Land. Several strongholds of independent Languedoc were mentioned, especially Penne d'Albigeois in the valley of the Aveyron, which took up the whole of article 31.

Raymond's father, Raymond VI, before betraying his people and joining the Crusade against the Cathars, underwent public humiliation at the

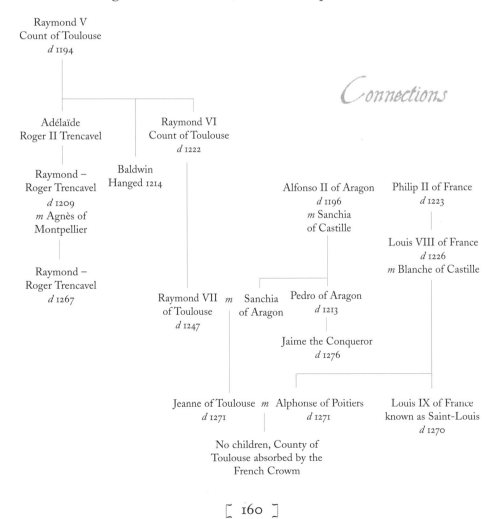

church of Saint-Gilles. Raymond VII was now required to do the same, but in Paris on the piazza in front of the cathedral of Notre-Dame. Like the defenders expelled from Carcassonne, he was required to strip to his undershirt and braies and go barefoot to listen to the articles of the treaty read aloud in the presence of the whole court of France, the papal legates and, among other clerics, the bishops of Narbonne and Toulouse.

Roger-Bernard of Foix, confident of his impregnable Pyrenean fortress, chose to reconcile himself with the French crown and accept the new status quo. Raymond Trencavel and a large number of dispossessed *co-seigneurs* of Languedoc loyal to him chose safety in exile in Aragon. Only Raymond's daughter Jeanne stood between the noble county and oblivion. On her death – she and Louis' younger brother, Alphonse of Poitiers, would have no children – all of Raymond's domains would revert to the French crown.

The Cathar church would have to fend for itself from now on; the independence of the house of Toulouse had been signed away.

CHAPTER 40

The 'Safe Mountain'

*I*n Lauragais, Minervois, Carcassès and Corbières, Catharism was now a guerrilla church. Some eminent Cathar priests, like Guilhabert of Castres, remained visible to the faithful through their tireless travelling and preaching, but fewer and fewer Cathars lived openly. This was a success for Rome. Before the Crusade began, Guilhabert shared a house with his sisters in Fanjeaux and must many times have passed Domingo de Guzmán, the founder of the Dominicans, in the narrow streets. Caught between the twin pincers of French crown and Catholic persecution, he – and his fellow priests – took to the woods and byways.

But this gave them a problem. Like many other Christian monks and nuns, one of the vows of the Cathar *parfait* was to live in 'community'. In fact, it was one of the great strengths of the Cathar church that their communities functioned so smoothly in the hearts of the towns and villages of Languedoc, a last quiet refuge for a widow or widower, a spiritual home for a devoted younger believer. There were separate houses for male and female Cathars, but Cathars readily admitted to living sometimes together in mixed households – and were mocked for it by Catholics whose judgemental cast of mind simply couldn't conceive of an honestly celibate community of women and men.

Of course, the Cathars taught that all souls were 'good and equal, one with another, and only Satan made a difference between their tunics of flesh'. There are records of female Bogomil priests from the 10th century and, in the registers of inquisitional interrogations, till the 14th century in Languedoc and the Pyrenees. Before the Crusade, there were perhaps almost as many *Bonnes Femmes* as *Bons Hommes* in the southwest, living by the labour of their hands in open orders, freely communicating with the world around them. Women were entitled to preach and 'save souls' just as men were, although the only records of them ordaining new priests through the *consolament* are of other women. There is no record of any female Cathar bishop, *filius major* or *filius minor*.

As the persecutions increased, the Cathars began to leave the open houses of their order in the *castra* of Languedoc, but had somehow to maintain the rule of community life. They did this by travelling always in pairs, a more experienced *parfait* or *parfaite* with a newer ordinand. As so often, they were no different in this from the Catholics who persecuted them, who also travelled in pairs. Even the papal legates – from Peter of Castelnau onwards – always had a companion, as would, later, the bloodthirsty bureaucrats of the Inquisition. Among the Dominicans – who condemned so many 'heretics' to imprisonment and death, never carrying out the sentences themselves but 'handing them over to the secular arm' – it was acknowledged that the two travelling brothers could always be on hand to give one another absolution. This might also have been a motivation for the pairs of itinerant Cathars.

Like the Cathars' vow of honesty, the obligation to live in community made life increasingly difficult as the net of persecution closed around them. They were more obvious – easier to spot by informers – travelling robed in pairs, praying and fasting regularly, declining to eat meat and so on. In the registers of the Inquisition and other contemporary documents, the Latin words '*socia*' and '*socius*' are used for, respectively, female and male 'companions'. In Occitan, they were – and are – called '*sòcia*' and '*sòci*'.

When a *sòcia* or *sòci* died or was taken by the Crusaders, a replacement of the appropriate sex needed to be found for the *parfait* or *parfaite* who remained. Around 1240, a devoted son called Raymond Raseire learnt that his mother, an itinerant, hounded *Bonne Femme*, had lost her *sòcia*. He took his sister to her so that his mother should ordain her through the *consolament* and be able to continue her ministry. They were both later burnt.

Also around this time, an itinerant Cathar *parfait* was living in an area of woodland in the plains of Lauragais between Toulouse and Carcassonne. His bag has been found. It contained a shirt, some bread, some wine, a few chickpeas and twenty-seven fresh eels. Perhaps he and his *sòci* had fished for them in the streams of the hills, or perhaps a generous believer had given them in return for a blessing, or to ensure that when their last days came, a *parfait* might be on hand to ensure that they could 'make a good end'. Perhaps the *Bon Homme* dropped the bag when he was taken – his skeleton was not found alongside.

As they hid in their low houses in the damp bracken at the foot of the forest trees, the guerrilla priests of the Cathar church reflected that this was, in a way, the natural order. They often asserted that persecution by the 'powers of the material world' was suffered by Christ and was a mark of distinction. In fact, they proclaimed that all who had power to see must recognise that the church of Rome couldn't be the true church of Christ, because of its regime of persecution.

But, by 1232, persecution was becoming more and more successful. Now Cathar bishop of Toulouse, Guilhabert of Castres realised that there was nowhere on the plains – not even Cabaret, Carcassonne or Fanjeaux – that could provide a secure home for the hierarchy of his church. He must have discussed the question of a suitable safe headquarters with his fellow Cathar priests. It would have been natural for them to look upwards, to the sharp-toothed chain of the Pyrenees, clearly visible in autumn, winter and spring before disappearing into the heat haze of summer.

Montségur

From the flat lands of Lauragais, one of the highest visible peaks is Saint-Barthélémy, at over 2,000 metres above sea level. In a valley below Saint-Barthélémy is a *pog* – a 'rocky mountain' – of about 1,200 metres, invisible from the plains, impregnably steep, gloriously isolated. Today, it is the only Pyrenean summit to go by the name of *pog* – a corruption of an old Occitan word. On top was a *château* – not the 14th-century castle that now stands there, but an older *castrum* owned by Raymond of Péreille.

That *castrum* was Montségur, the 'safe mountain'. It would become their refuge. Signposted from the plains by mighty Saint-Barthélémy, it must have served as a constant reminder to the persecuted faithful that they were not alone – at least not yet.

⌘ CHAPTER 41 ⌘
Mirepoix and Péreille

M irepoix today is a charming late-medieval *bastide* – a fortified
town built on a square grid of streets. At its centre is a large
rectangular *place*, surrounded on three sides by timbered
colonnades.

Ancient timber-built houses in modern Mirepoix.

On the ground floor are shops and restaurants, shaded by the verandas formed by the substantial wooden posts that support the overhanging rooms of the homes above. On the south side of the *place* is the church, previously the cathedral of Saint-Maurice.

The building of this picturesque *bastide* was only begun in 1279, after the original town was flooded when a dam burst at Puivert in the Pyrenees. In 1967, part of an old set of floorboards in the bishop's tribune in Mirepoix was removed in order to carry out repairs. Beneath the floorboards was a paved subfloor of painted ceramic tiles, dated to about 1530 CE. An area of tiles around 60 centimetres square illustrated a labyrinth with, to one side, a picture of a Minotaur.

The city of Mirepoix existed in Gallo-Roman times – the first centuries after Christ – but there is no trace of any fortifications until the 10th century. At the same time, there is a record of the sale of a vineyard just outside the walls. In the 11th century, the local *seigneurs* paid homage to both Foix and Carcassonne. In 1104, Roger of Mirepoix died in Jerusalem, fighting alongside the count of Foix in the First Crusade.

A decade before the start of the Crusade against the Cathars, there were at least fifty 'houses of heretics' in Mirepoix and the records of the Inquisition state that in 1206 the city welcomed a Cathar council with at least 500 or even 600 members.

At the time of the council, the most important of the thirty-five *co-seigneurs* of Mirepoix was Pierre-Roger, whose entire family were Cathar believers. In 1204, he thought himself mortally wounded and travelled to Fanjeaux to be consoled by Guilhabert of Castres. But he survived until 1209, consoled this time by a local Cathar priest, and was succeeded by his son, Pierre-Roger the Younger. Later that year, fresh from victory at Carcassonne, Mirepoix was taken by Simon of Montfort. Pierre-Roger the Younger was *faydit* – dispossessed. Three years later, Montfort was looking for suitable territories to grant his faithful ally Guy of Lévis. He chose an area of around 200 square kilometres, perhaps including Montségur, with Mirepoix as its capital.

At the turn of the 13th century, Montségur was a ruined outpost belonging to the nearby *seigneurs* of Péreille. Around 1200, Fournière of Péreille left her husband to become a Cathar, living in a community of Cathar women. About four years later, her son, Raymond, was asked by the Cathar church hierarchy to rebuild the *castrum*. He agreed and, having done so, he chose to take up residence there rather than live in the *château* at

Péreille. He married – Corba – and they had a daughter – Esclarmonde.

Montfort died in 1218 at the siege of Toulouse. In 1222, as Montfort's son Amaury was losing all his father's conquests one by one, Raymond-Roger of Foix besieged Mirepoix, but the troops of Louis VIII's Royal Crusade soon took it back. The next year, another siege, led by Foix and the *faydit* Pierre-Roger of Mirepoix the Younger, was successful and the Cathar church quickly re-established itself in the town.

Around 1227, Guilhabert of Castres himself became deacon of Mirepoix. Then, in 1229, Raymond VII of Toulouse signed away all his rights in Languedoc to the French crown. It was increasingly dangerous for the persecuted church to spread its message of universal salvation. Around 1231, the inquisitor Ferrier was told: 'Melina, a mother of three brothers from Pradelles…received the *consolament* from the *Bons Chrétiens* because she was ill. But she recovered and left the village of Pradelles and built a hut in the woods and lived there outside the village, for three or four years.'

Because of the widespread presence of inquisitors and informers, the *Bons Chrétiens* moved out of the towns and villages and into the forests and hills, moving in secret two by two, often under cover of night. They had taken vows of poverty – along with chastity, truth-telling, vegetarianism and so forth – that obliged them to earn a living from their own labours and not simply rely on charity. They were proud that they were not a burden on their believers. Often they worked as weavers, a highly portable trade that could be accommodated by their itinerant preaching. Others were needlemakers or tailors, but a still more common trade seems to have been the making of combs – sometimes called cards – used for teasing out the knotted wool collected from sheep or goats and making it ready for spinning.

Many female priests fulfilled the vow for manual labour by sewing or spinning wool or thread for tailoring work. In the darkest times, hidden away in low houses in the damp forest, a few *Bonnes Chrétiennes* were exploited by their supposed protectors who obliged them to work night and day in payment for their meagre meals.

Believers would be kept informed of the presence of the itinerant Cathar priests. Sometimes they would be accompanied for their protection by a *faydit* – a dispossessed knight of Languedoc, from Cabaret or Montréal or elsewhere. Low houses of wood and stone were built in clearings in the trees or tucked in a fold of the land. Occasionally the Cathar priests would enter a village after dark and knock quietly at a friendly door. Now and then, a messenger would be sent to their last known location to say that they were needed, that some poor soul was dying and wished to 'make a good end' and requested the consolation of faith.

Guilhabert of Castres was by now Cathar bishop of Toulouse. In the midst of this increasing persecution, he asked Raymond of Péreille for permission to move the seat of his diocese to the Péreille family's Pyrenean stronghold of Montségur.

At this time, the *castrum* of Montségur was a fortified village, much more extensive than today's castle. The houses backed on to one another for protection and support, and a large area of the mountaintop itself was terraced to make it habitable. At the centre of the *castrum* was a substantial tower, but nothing like the ruins that occupy the *pog* today.

Raymond agreed. In 1232, the 'safe mountain' became the Cathars' last refuge. For good and for ill, Pierre-Roger of Mirepoix became leader of its garrison.

⌘ CHAPTER 42 ⌘
The Inquisition

*I*n the early Middle Ages, crimes were sometimes judged by making the accused undergo an ordeal, usually by water or by fire. If the accused survived drowning or recovered from their burns, they were deemed to be innocent – unless, that is, they were judged to have received assistance from the Devil. The Crusaders exported ordeals to the Holy Land, where they bemused the Muslim Usamah. He wrote in his autobiography of 1175:

*T*hey installed a huge cask and filled it with water. Across it they set a board of wood. They then bound the arms of the man charged with the act, tied a rope around his shoulders and dropped him into the cask, their idea being that if he was innocent, he would sink in the water and they would then lift him up with the rope so that he might not die; if he was guilty, he would not sink in the water. This man did his best to sink when they dropped him into the water, but he could not do it. So he had to submit to their sentence against him – may Allah's curse be upon them! They pierced his eyeballs with red-hot awls.

From this low base, the quasi-judicial process of investigation by the Inquisition was a relative improvement.

The constant threat hang-

A 13th-century sentence of mutilation is carried out.

ing over Toulouse and other opponents of the Catholic church was excommunication – and, with it, loss of feudal and property rights. But the Cathar priests had virtually no property and couldn't give two hoots for the other strictures: forbidden to enter a church, forbidden to receive the sacraments, forbidden burial in hallowed ground and so on.

So, in 1229, the Catholic Council of Toulouse decreed that in each parish a priest and two or three laymen should seek out 'heretics' and destroy their dwellings and property. Any who allowed 'heretics' to dwell on their land should lose it. Houses where 'heretics' were discovered were to be pulled down. Laymen were forbidden to own the Bible's Old or New Testaments and Occitan translations of holy books were forbidden. 'Heretics' were forbidden to act as doctors.

Four years later, Pope Gregory IX gave responsibility for the developing Inquisition to the Dominican order. One of Guzmán's earliest companions, Pierre Sellan, had given his own home in Toulouse to the Dominican order. In 1234, Sellan became one of the very first inquisitors to be appointed by the pope and his house became the headquarters of the Inquisition in the *ville rose*. Alongside him was the Catholic lawyer Guillaume Arnaut.

A local bishop might dispute with the Dominicans the right to try a 'heretic' – and, therefore, the right to sequester the victim's property. The inquisitors consistently asserted the authority of the pope to maintain their mandate. At the same time, they refused to take proper responsibility for the executions they caused to take place. The vows of the Dominicans and Cistercians who made up the Inquisition forbade them from causing the deaths of their victims. Throughout their brutal campaign, they preserved a fig-leaf of Christian charity over their judicial torture and murder, insisting euphemistically that a defiant Cathar priest who would not abjure or a relapsed believer should be 'handed over to the secular arm'. The 'secular arm' might be a local landowner or a member of the Crusader army or an agent of the French king. These 'seculars' sometimes competed for the right to burn because it also gave them the right to a portion of the victim's estate.

Inquisitorial registers began to be compiled, copious archives of two aspects of the Inquisition's work – the interrogations and the accusations of informers, the sentences of the inquisitors. Both represent an extraordinary mine of historical data, even though it all has to be handled with caution. The register was, after all, compiled by Catholics about 'heretics'. A good example of this is the way the *melhorament* – the Cathars' ritual greeting – was infallibly transcribed as 'adoration', deliberately trying to throw an unpleasant idolatrous light on the innocent practice of asking for a priest's blessing. In one testimony, a suspect told the inquisitor: 'I gave them bread but I never adored them.' She was imprisoned.

The Inquisition interrogated at exhaustive length in punishing detail. (The Toulouse register contains more than 5,600 statements collected by the investigation of Bernard of Caux alone.) Each testimony was carefully recorded by a notary or scribe. Each time a suspect was questioned, just as important as their confession was the collection of evidence against other – as yet unsuspected – Cathars. The same questions and the same answers came back time and again: 'Did you adore the heretics? Did you take food to the heretics? Did you listen to the heretics? Did you believe the heretics?'

To encourage informers the Inquisition nurtured a climate of fear. The accused had legal representation, but generally of only a symbolic kind. In any case, advocates who defended their charges too well – like Guillaume Garric of Carcassonne – were suspected of 'heresy' in their turn.

Carts loaded with 'heretics' trundled towards the flames. Sometimes the buildings in which 'heretic' ceremonies had taken place would be condemned and demolished. The building plot was then supposed to lie fallow for a century in order for it to become clean. The bodies of people suspected of dying in the Cathar faith were exhumed and placed alongside the living on the pyres.

At first, the purpose of the Inquisition was to convert and then impose penitence. After all, the practices of investigation and trial had been carried out – almost exclusively by Cistercians – without the name or authority of the Inquisition for about fifty years. But, in this new official phase, the goal was no longer to convert, nor was it designed simply to cleanse the living community of 'heresy' – the purpose was to impose an eternal punishment. The point of burning bodies and exhumed corpses was to ensure that they could not resuscitate on Judgment Day.

The Inquisition imposed a carefully graduated set of punishments. A 'heretic' who recanted and embraced the Catholic faith once more could expect leniency; if they then relapsed – reverted to Catharism – they would immediately be sought out and burnt, without question or delay. (Sometimes infidels – Jews or Muslims – would be investigated, but only if they had converted to Catholicism and then relapsed.) At the same time, rules were framed to protect informers: 'The names of witnesses are to be kept secret. However, an accused person may list the names of his enemies…In a case of heresy any person whatsoever may be admitted as accuser or witness, not excluding criminals, evil-livers or their accomplices.'

The accused *Bons Chrétiens* had the opportunity to abjure their faith – a solemn renunciation to the tribunal of their 'heretical' beliefs. Even Cathar priests could escape the flames in this way and their sentence would be commuted to life imprisonment. There were a number of higher Cathar dignitaries who abjured and were accepted directly into the Catholic hierarchy as priests or canons.

Out of reach of the inquisitors, in the high citadel of Montségur and other safe places, the Cathar bishops continued their work, ordaining new *Bons Chrétiens* and dispatching them two by two into the hills. But if one was taken, others would follow because, even in the inquisitorial court, they were obliged to tell the truth. Several Cathars were condemned when they admitted their 'heresy' rather than slaughter an animal brought for that purpose into the tribunal. In one inquisitorial testimony appears the story of a *Bon Homme* who was taken when he stopped outside an abattoir to weep for the souls of the butchers.

On 4 August 1234, Domingo de Guzmán was canonised. In Toulouse on the same day, the Dominican friar Raimon du Fauga organised a strange sort of celebration. He had heard from an informer that an old woman at death's door had recently been visited by a Cathar priest who had recited for her the *consolament* – the consoling prayer that would enable her soul to return to God. He took off his black cowl and the other insignia of his vicious authority and attended the old woman disguised as a Cathar. Believing herself in the presence of a holy man, the woman confessed her faith. Raimon had the woman and her cot carried out into the street and quickly burnt, so as not to allow her the mercy of dying before the flames could consume her. The Dominican community of Toulouse then celebrated the twin accomplishments of the woman's pyre and the canonisation of their founder with a joyful meal.

Under the pressure of the court, patterns of belief within families were sundered. Irlande de Villèle told her inquisitor: 'Because my mother-in-law, Ava, kept asking me to, for two days I believed the heretics were *Bons Hommes* and true Friends of God, but no longer than that…and I never saw the heretics again or ever adored them again, even though my mother-in-law kept asking me to.'

The family of Guilhem Authié from Villepinte was one of thousands destroyed by the Inquisition:

My father, Raimon Authié, and my mother, Raimonde, his wife, both became heretics. Then…they were converted and reconciled with the Catholic faith by Saint Dominic and the Abbot of Villelongue, and received their letters of reconciliation. But my mother, Raimonde, returned to her vomit, became a heretic once more and was burnt. But I never knelt before her and never gave or sent her anything.

In 1235 in Lombardy in northern Italy, two years on from the foundation of the Inquisition, an Italian Cathar exclaimed:

'Look at them! They have killed those who will not swear oaths or fornicate or eat meat…but against those who march with a sword at their side and commit adultery and murder, they do nothing. Church of Rome, your hands are drenched with the blood of martyrs!'

CHAPTER 43
Knowledge of Hell

*L*egend tells us that Heracles – Hercules in the Roman tradition – came to the land between France and Spain when resting after the tenth of his twelve labours – the theft of the oxen of Geryon. He created the stone Pillars of Hercules delimiting the Mediterranean at the Strait of Gibraltar. He then travelled north and accepted the hospitality of King Bebryx and his beautiful daughter, Pyrène.

Heracles and Pyrène spent the night together but, the following morning, Heracles left before sunrise to begin leading the golden-horned oxen home to Greece. Pyrène woke alone and set out after him. In the darkness of the forest, she was torn to pieces by wild wolves. On learning this dreadful news, Heracles, in grief and rage, collected up the mightiest, most beautiful rocks he could find and piled them up in an immeasurable monument to the tender, beautiful and loving woman with whom he had spent just one night. In doing so, he created the Pyrenean mountain range.

If you visit the Pyrenees today, you can penetrate deep underground at Lombrives and visit the Tomb of Pyrène, a vast open cavern deep below the mountain at whose centre stands an opalescent rock in the shape of a rough sarcophagus. From the roof, high above, falls a constant drip-drop of water

The Tombe de Pyrène

seeping through the limestone, forever renewing the tomb. In fact, the *Tombe de Pyrène* is the only chamber in the whole huge network of caverns and caves where, regardless of drought or season on the summits, the Pyrenees never stop weeping.

In the time of persecution, it must have seemed to the Cathars that, truly, the world was created for misery and suffering by the Devil himself. There was no need of another – spiritual – Hell.

Most human societies have a vision of an afterlife. It seems to be a way of coping with the fact that life is a matter of chance, an unfathomable coincidence. That being so, then there must be something else – a place of reward, for example – when life is done. And because life is – often – unfair, people seek a logic or rationale behind the unpredicted event, the poor harvest, the broken wheel or the stillborn child. So we develop an ingrained sense of the deserving and the undeserving, the right to salvation and the entitlement to punishment.

In response, the Cathars, of course, laughed. The soul, being divine, cannot be destroyed. It is, most Christians agree, an 'immortal' soul. On the other hand, the body will die and rot. It is subject to corruption, like meat or a fallen tree. For the Cathars, this was a sign – a clue – that the body could not have been created by God, who was wholly good, wholly divine, wholly incorruptible. Nothing, they believed, that died could come from God. All that died – that faded, that declined, that wore away like the rocks of the mountains or failed to endure like a rusted knife – was created by Satan. All that God made was the souls, eternal, enduring, tricked out of Heaven and imprisoned in 'tunics of flesh'. So God sent Jesus to remind us of our heavenly home, to offer us knowledge of the way back to God's side – by 'making a good end', consoled by the blessing of the Cathar priest reciting the supersubstantial Word of God: 'In the beginning was the Word, and the Word was with God and the Word was God.'

Because of this revelation – this sense of a hidden destiny concealed by Satan – some people believe that the Cathars were gnostics, that they believed in a path to enlightenment through knowledge. This is not so.

Gnosis is Greek for 'knowledge'. (An 'agnostic', on the other hand, 'does not know'.) There were Christian gnostics in Egypt and Syria in the first centuries after Christ and they developed a complex web of revelations, some tied solely to Christianity, others drawing on pre-Christian myths. Some of them were dualists, believing in a world divided into good and evil. They were condemned as 'heretics' by the emerging Catholic church in the

3rd and 4th centuries, but they didn't pass their tradition down through the Bogomils to the Cathars. There was no complexity in Cathar teaching, no difficult path to enlightenment, no esoteric, concealed knowledge that must be decoded from ancient texts. The Cathars were not gnostics. There was just the Word and the eventual certainty of a return to God.

Because the material world was created by Satan and had nothing of God in it, the Cathars did not believe that Christ was ever made flesh – that he was 'God made man'. They taught that he appeared to humankind and appeared to die on the cross – but he did not do so in reality. God, for the Cathars, could not take material form. But the lesson of Christ's symbolic sacrifice was accepted by Cathar teaching and the *Bons Chrétiens* themselves promised to imitate his example and accept martyrdom 'in this base world'.

Because the Cathars believed that the death of the body was an opportunity – a moment when the soul might be free to return to Heaven – some people say they sought death. But that isn't true either. The Cathars had plenty of opportunity to end their days by giving themselves up to the Inquisition – but they did not do so. They endured dreadful hardship in their clandestine ministry in order to continue their work of consoling and comforting their flock.

Because of the Cathar regime of fasting, some people say that they sought death through starvation. This isn't true either, but it is an understandable mistake. Many Cathars were consoled on their death beds and, once the ceremony was complete, they were obliged to fast on bread and water. If they failed to keep to this meagre diet, the *consolament* would become void. Seeing this, the Inquisition mistakenly assumed they were deliberately starving themselves to death and, in the inquisitional register of interrogations they used the Occitan word *endura* – meaning 'test' – to describe their harsh fast.

Self-starvation was used as a political tool. Late on in their genocide of the Cathars, the monks of the Inquisition felt obliged to construct 'emergency' pyres to burn alive *parfaits* – such as Jacques Authié or Amiel of Perles – who protested their innocence by hunger strike. For the Dominicans and Cistercians of the Catholic church's Inquisition, it was important that the 'heretics' should burn alive.

The Cathar priesthood was non-violent and relied on others to protect them through strength of arms. They forbade murder and opposed the death penalty for any crime. Unlike the Catholic church of the Middle Ages, they declined to create exceptions to this rule for Jews or Muslims.

They were trapped. There was no easy way. They had an obligation to respect their vows and a duty to spread the Word. Unwilling to lie, unwilling to fight, the Cathars could only hide.

▣ CHAPTER 44 ▣
The Beginning of the End

*I*n early 1233, Pope Gregory IX commanded an inquisitional investigation to be carried out into the Niort family. Esclarmonde, the wife of the viscount, told the inquisitor: 'My faith is better than your faith, better than that of any of the priests of This World.'

Troops of the Royal Crusade were sent to the plateau of Sault and attacked the Niort castle at Roquefeuil, without success. The Niort forces were supported by Pierre-Roger of Mirepoix and other dispossessed *seigneurs* of Languedoc.

Only a few ancient stones suggest the outline of a room in the ruins of the château *at Roquefeuil.*

Under pressure from Rome and Paris, Raymond VII published an 'anti-heretic' edict. The punishments – confiscation of property, open prison, closed prison, death – touched more and more families. Bogus informers came forward. In Toulouse, an artisan accused of 'heresy' complained to the consuls that this was slander. The consuls fined the neighbour who accused him, but the neighbour appealed to the inquisitors, who overturned the verdict of the democratic representatives. The artisan fled the city, finding refuge in Lombardy. Another Toulousain – who denied being a Cathar – couldn't be burnt because a spontaneous crowd prevented it. He was imprisoned with a number of *parfaits* captured in Lavaur. When the time came for the Lavaur *Bons Chrétiens* to be burnt, the Toulousain had converted to Catharism and he was executed on the same pyre.

At the beginning of 1235, the Dominicans organised a vast festival of preaching, confession and absolution. Their idea was to make a list of those who did not attend. So many people bowed to the pressure to take part that the Dominican inquisitors had to ask for assistance from Cistercians and church priests. A man named Arnaud Domergue failed to attend confession and was arrested. To avoid capital punishment, he gave away the location of seven *parfaits* from Cassès who were taken and burnt in his stead. Then he himself was killed in the middle of the night.

Public discontent grew louder. Raymond VII of Toulouse became worried and replaced his *viguier* – his bailiff or administrator – with a man he thought more likely to be able to moderate the excesses of the Dominicans. The inquisitor Guillaume Arnaut summoned to trial a list of twelve known 'heretics' but was expelled from the city before they could be heard. He wrote from Carcassonne to his brothers in the *ville rose*, demanding that they continue the hearings. On the night of 5 November 1235, the soldiers of the Toulouse militia expelled the forty Dominican inquisitors who were resident in the city. On 11 November, Guillaume Arnaut excommunicated Raymond VII and eleven of the city's consuls.

Two Dominicans made the long journey to Rome to explain what had happened. Pope Gregory IX wrote to Raymond to remind him of his obligations – the unfulfilled payment of reparations to the Catholic church, his own unprepared departure for five years to the Holy Land at Easter 1237. He also wrote to the French king, Louis IX, now twenty-one years old, asking him to exert pressure on Toulouse. Raymond responded by visiting Guillaume Arnaut in Carcassonne and negotiating the return of the inquisitors to his capital. He managed to exclude the Dominican zealot

Pierre Sellan and had him replaced by a more moderate Franciscan.

In February 1237, the Niort family was summoned once more to the inquisitional tribunal, this time in Carcassonne. Statements were taken from 140 witnesses. Guillaume Arnaut sentenced five of them – including Esclarmonde – to life imprisonment. In the same year, Jeanne of Toulouse, Raymond and Sanchia of Aragon's daughter, married the brother of Louis IX, Alphonse of Poitiers. Whatever happened next, the house of Toulouse would eventually be absorbed into the French crown.

The investigations continued. Raymond's administrator in Quercy, in the north of his lands, took advantage of a short amnesty to admit to the inquisitors his 'heretic' beliefs. He was condemned to support a poor peasant for the remainder of his days and, before Easter 1239, accomplish pilgrimages to Saint-Gilles – where Peter of Castelnau was briefly interred – Compostela and elsewhere. In April 1237, a rare conversion of the *parfait* Raymond Gros led to a 'miraculous number of arrests'. Another Cathar, Alaman of Rouaix, was sentenced to life imprisonment, but no one could be found to arrest him and he carried on living and preaching in the streets of Toulouse. A new Inquisition was set up to seek out 'heretics' in the kingdom of Aragon and *Bons Chrétiens* living and dead were burnt in the Pyrenean lands of the count of Foix.

Throughout this period of persecution, Raymond VII worked diplomatically to alleviate the burden of the Treaty of Paris. His departure for the Holy Land was put back to 24 June. His complaints to the pope about the conduct of the Inquisition were passed on to Guillaume Arnaut by Rome and, once more, the over-zealous inquisitors were instructed to restrict themselves to the letter of the law. But Raymond still could not obtain permission to bury his father's remains in hallowed ground.

Then, on 20 May 1237, Gregory IX lost patience or decided that he had nothing further to gain from accommodating the desires of Toulouse. He wrote to Louis IX, itemising Raymond's derogations to the Treaty of Paris. But the pope had misjudged their relative strengths and Raymond refused to back down. In fact, he used the crisis to his advantage and had the date of his Crusade to the Holy Land deferred indefinitely. The excommunications of 1235 – when the inquisitors were expelled from Toulouse – were lifted from both himself and the eleven consuls.

In February 1238, thirty-five Toulousains believed to have recanted then resumed their 'heretic practices' were sentenced to life imprisonment. In May, a new papal legate came into office and the Inquisition was suspended for three months, then for a further six months awaiting his arrival. The legate failed to turn up in France and was replaced once more. Raymond met the new appointment and negotiated the release of a number of life prisoners against the payment of reparations to the University of Toulouse.

The following year, 1239, Raymond continued to undermine the work of the inquisitor. In Provence – where the house of Toulouse had many possessions – he was drawn into conflict on the orders of Frederic II, the Holy Roman Emperor and his suzerain in southeastern France. (Frederic's empire – the descendant of Charlemagne's great realm – was frequently at war with the papal states and he was twice excommunicated by Rome. At one point, Gregory IX declared he was the Antichrist.) Raymond was once more excommunicated, but the intervention of the kings of France and Britain defused the crisis.

On Raymond's return to Languedoc in August, he was met by the royal seneschal of Carcassonne. He was perhaps surprised to discover that the seneschal wanted his help in putting down a rebellion.

The rebellion was led by Raymond Trencavel, now thirty-two years old and determined to regain his family's lands and titles. Alongside him were virtually all the celebrated *faydits*, including Olivier of Termes, Guillaume of Peyrepertuse, Chabert of Barbaira, Guillaume of Minerve, Pierre-Roger of Mirepoix and Géraud of Niort. Their goal was to retake the Cité on the Hill.

⚎ CHAPTER 45 ⚎
The Return of Trencavel

aymond Trencavel, the son of Raymond-Roger Trencavel and Agnès of Montpellier, was two years old when Carcassonne fell to the *Ost gran* in 1209. His father, Raymond-Roger, was imprisoned and died in a dungeon of the Cité. Simon of Montfort then persuaded Agnès to sign away her rights and those of her young son for a steady pension and the return of her dowry. Raymond became the ward of Raymond-Roger of Foix and spent much of his time in exile in Aragon.

Soon after the fall of Carcassonne, in November 1210, the *château* of Termes fell to Montfort's siege. Olivier of Termes was only ten years old at the time of the catastrophe. His inheritance was appropriated and given to one of Montfort's lieutenants, but he escaped and became a *faydit* – a dispossessed knight. He fled across the Pyrenees and became a close friend and ally of Raymond Trencavel, Raymond the Younger of Toulouse and of the son of Pedro of Aragon. He entered the service of all three, fighting the armies of the French king for Trencavel, Toulouse and the Cathar church and taking part in the conquest of the Moors of Majorca with the army of Aragon.

Montfort died in 1218. On 14 January 1224, Montfort's son Amaury – after losing virtually all of the possessions his father had so brilliantly conquered – signed a document of surrender at Carcassonne. The next day, Raymond Trencavel slept in the Château Comtal of his ancestors.

On 25 August 1224, Raymond of Toulouse and Raymond-Roger of Foix each swore an oath to eradicate 'heresy' from their lands and pay reparations to the Catholic churches. At the same time, Catharism flourished and the French king, Louis VIII, marched south with a new army. Trencavel and Foix fled Carcassonne and established a command post in Limoux, which became *faydite* itself – a rebel city.

A French manuscript illumination, c.1325–1350 showing sappers in action.

In April 1227, a Catholic council in Narbonne pronounced a sentence of excommunication on Toulouse, Foix and Trencavel. In June, as the situation worsened, Trencavel wrote a will that made Foix the heir to his lands and rights. In 1228, he fled once more over the mountains into Aragon. Soon after, in 1229, Raymond of Toulouse signed the disastrous Treaty of Paris and all of Trencavel's rights were claimed by the French crown. Olivier of Termes was still in Languedoc, protecting Cathar preachers from patrols, carrying messages to their remote hideaways and bringing them to havens in the homes of the faithful.

In exile, Raymond Trencavel never abandoned hoped of regaining his lands. In 1239, Amaury of Montfort left France for the Holy Land on the count of Champagne's Crusade, abandoning his title of count of Toulouse to the king of France. Did that encourage Trencavel? In late summer 1240, he arrived in Languedoc accompanied by a roll-call of virtually every well-known *faydit* knight, including Olivier of Termes, Géraud of Niort and Pierre-Roger of Mirepoix. An army of local people, no doubt fired with thoughts of revenge for the grotesque conduct of the Inquisition, joined him. One after another the towns and villages fell: Montréal, Saissac, Montolieu.

In early September, Trencavel's rebellion occupied the Carcassonne suburb of Saint-Vincent. Despite the complicity of some of the population of the Cité, he failed to penetrate the walls and was obliged to establish a siege. The seneschal of Carcassonne managed to send word to Louis IX, king of France, who promised reinforcements. The seneschal prepared to hold the Cité until then.

Trencavel deployed his sappers. They chose seven different positions in which to attempt to undermine the fortifications, 'digging like moles'. They began their tunnels inside the houses that backed on to the walls, protecting themselves from attack. Within the Cité, the defenders built palisades inside the battlements in case the stonework collapsed. They dug their own tunnels in an attempt to intercept Trencavel's sappers. Strange subterranean combats ensued, using 'hand weapons, smoke and quick lime'.

Louis IX's army of reinforcements came in sight and still Trencavel had been unable to penetrate the Cité. On 11 October, he instructed his men to set fire to the suburb, burning several houses of Catholic monks and the convent of Sainte-Marie, before fleeing to the hill town of Montréal, 20 kilometres west. Louis's army followed and besieged the young viscount. Ladies of the local Languedoc nobility joined in the defence of the town.

Several *parfaits*, including the Cathar bishop of Carcassonne, were smuggled away by three of the *faydits*.

The counts of Toulouse and Foix sent word to Trencavel, advising him to negotiate. The spontaneous army was at first allowed to disband. The town of Montréal – and others that supported the brief rebellion – were razed to the ground. A number of suspected 'heretics' were branded with a hot iron cross on their foreheads.

Louis' army followed the *faydits* into the hills. The rearguard was taken and several knights hanged. High in the Corbières, Olivier of Termes was forced to surrender at Laroque-de-Fa, the end of his long war of revenge and resistance. Then Peyrepertuse fell and Géraud of Niort was taken. On 13 December 1240, Géraud pledged allegiance to Louis IX of France and negotiated the release of his mother, Esclarmonde, and brothers from imprisonment. But the Niort family possessions on the plateau of Sault he had to abandon to the crown of France.

Raymond Trencavel slipped away over the mountains into Aragon once more.

⊞ CHAPTER 46 ⊞

The Murders at Avignonet

The position of Raymond VII of Toulouse was less and less secure. Officially, Amaury of Montfort had inherited the title from his father, Simon, who took it by conquest. Amaury renounced it, in 1239, in favour of the French king, before leaving for the Holy Land. He fought recklessly and was taken prisoner. After eighteen months in prison in Cairo, his health suffered and he died soon after his release on his return journey in 1241. The Montfort family had finally finished with Languedoc.

Of course, Raymond had failed, yet again, to respect the punitive clauses of the Treaty of Paris. So he sent a troop of soldiers of Toulouse to Montségur to enact a bogus siege. Nothing came of it and it is unlikely either France or Rome was convinced. At the same time, Raymond tried – without much success – to have the more moderate bishops take over the role of inquisitors from the Dominicans.

Languedoc was sinking beneath a vicious tide of judicial murders, flowing into the valleys and foothills of the Pyrenees, rising inexorably up the flanks of even the highest strongholds of the condemned Cathar church. Guillaume Arnaut and his brothers were tireless, interrogating, condemning, imprisoning and burning those who believed that God was good and Satan evil, that all souls would finally be saved and that eternal damnation was an invention of priests, designed to subdue their flocks.

Pierre-Roger of Mirepoix, the leader of the garrison at Montségur, received word of the arrival of a group of inquisitors in the small town of Avignonet on 28 May 1242. Perhaps he also received instruction to act from Raymond VII of Toulouse. In any case, he assembled a troop of perhaps fifty knights from the Montségur garrison, armed with swords and axes. With the astonishing stamina of medieval walkers, the soldiers covered the 85 kilometres to Avignonet, reinforced by twenty-five or thirty more soldiers on the way. They arrived only one day later, soon after the inquisitors had gone to bed on the evening of 29 May 1242.

Three knights and twelve *sergents* approached the castle. Someone crept in through a window and let everyone in. With accelerating excitement and fury, the doors to the inquisitors' bedrooms were smashed open. Four Dominicans – including Guillaume Arnaut – a Franciscan, an archdeacon and his clerk, two bailiffs, a priest and the tribunal scribe were hacked to death as the men of Montségur competed in vengeful violence.

Later, seven different men claimed to have struck the first blows. It is said that Guillaume Arnaut died with the *Te Deum* on his lips. His body was pierced by many swords, his head crushed on the stone floor, his inquisitorial records carried away and destroyed. Pierre-Roger of Mirepoix is supposed to have complained to his men that they should have brought him the inquisitor's skull to use as a goblet.

The ferocity and audacity of the massacre of the inquisitors at Avignonet brought a swift response. Raymond VII was once more excommunicated and his lands threatened. In October, he wrote to Louis IX to swear his loyalty, repeating his vow before the Catholic bishop of Toulouse and Imbert of Beaujeu, leader of the Crusader army in Languedoc. In January 1243, he signed a document reaffirming the Treaty of Paris. He married a close relative – Marguerite de la Marche – requesting papal dispensation. (He would never receive it.) He was desperate to show willing and had four of the Avignonet murderers captured. Three of them were hanged. He complained again to Rome of the behaviour of the Dominican inquisitors who acted above the law. In the summer, he travelled to Italy in order to negotiate with the new pope, Innocent IV. But Innocent responded by increasing the Dominicans' powers.

In any case, decisively, in the spring of 1243, the siege of Montségur had already begun.

⌘ CHAPTER 47 ⌘
The Siege of Montségur

*A*t the start of the siege of Montségur in late spring 1243, between 400 and 500 people were living on the mountaintop. There were nearly thirty members of the family of Raymond of Péreille, lord of the stronghold, of whom three of the women were *parfaites*. In addition to seven or eight servants of the Péreille household, there was a doctor – Arnaud Rouquier – and his wife and son. The garrison commanded by Pierre-Roger of Mirepoix included twelve knights, fifty-five *sergents*, a catapult expert, some other military personnel and many members of the soldiers' families.

Then, of course, there were at least 200 Cathar *parfaits* and *parfaites*. We know the names of forty-nine of them, thirty-four men and fifteen women, including the three Péreille family members. Their spiritual leader was Bertrand Marty, who had succeeded Guilhabert of Castres as Cathar bishop of Toulouse, accompanied by his *filius minor*. The Cathar bishop of Razès, Raymond Agulher, was also there, plus several Cathar deacons.

Before the siege encircled the mountain, there was constant traffic as the *Bons Chrétiens* left two by two on foot to spread the Word and the faithful climbed the steep slopes as pilgrims or carrying provisions. The community was purposeful and manual labour well organised. Two workshops – each with at least a hundred people – made clothes for soldiers and civilians. One *parfait* was a barber, another a cobbler, another a miller.

The siege was established by the seneschal – the royal governor – of Carcassonne, Hugues des Arcis. Like other royal appointees, the seneschal paid the king for the privilege of running the city and made sure he profited from the deal through extortion and corruption.

Hugues was an able tactician but, even supported by mercenaries, he did not have enough men to completely encircle the mountain. A partial siege was in place at the end of May. Hugues used his forces to compel local recruits whose loyalty was uncertain. The archbishop of Albi brought 150 men of his own. Though human traffic continued between the *pog* and the valleys, it quickly became difficult to bring in provisions. Fortunately for the defenders, the stores of the *castrum* were extremely well stocked.

As the summer progressed, just three of the defenders were killed, mortally wounded in skirmishes. Each was consoled by the *parfaits* before they succumbed. Despite the fact that losses were very light and although winter would surely soon come to their aid, Raymond of Péreille and Pierre-Roger of Mirepoix were concerned. They had learnt that the count of Foix had joined the Crusaders. They also knew that Raymond VII of Toulouse – realistically their only potential ally – was in Italy negotiating with the new pope. So they sent messengers to find out his plans. They crept out of the citadel and slipped away through the enemy lines. One of them signalled back by fire from a nearby mountaintop. The news was good – Raymond VII would be back in Languedoc by the end of the year.

By December Hugues des Arcis became worried in his turn. Soon his work would be hindered by snow. He decided he must act. A lightly armed group of Crusaders were led by local and Basque mercenaries up the dangerous Roc de la Tour, a spike of stone rising steeply at the easternmost point of the summit ridge of Montségur. It was an astonishing feat of daring, at night on the vertiginous terrain. Without the assistance of local men who knew the lie of the land, it would have been impossible. But they all made it to the summit of the Roc, killed the sentries and set up camp. When dawn broke and they looked back down the near-vertical drop to the jagged rocks below, they shook with fear.

The camp on the Roc de la Tour was about 750 metres from the *castrum* and 350 metres lower, but it brought the castle and its barbican in range of siege weapons. On the walls of Montségur, the defenders could only watch as the catapults and mangonels were winched up. The Crusader weapons engineers got busy. Mighty balls of rough-hewn stone were launched up to the summit. For those trapped inside, the noise of the bombardment was as effective in breaking their spirit as the physical damage inflicted on the walls. Bertrand Marty decided to take the precaution of evacuating the Cathar church's 'treasure'.

The word 'treasure' meant money. Despite this, over the years, legends surrounding what was smuggled out of the besieged citadel have grown. Perhaps, concealed within the treasury of gold and silver coins, was hidden

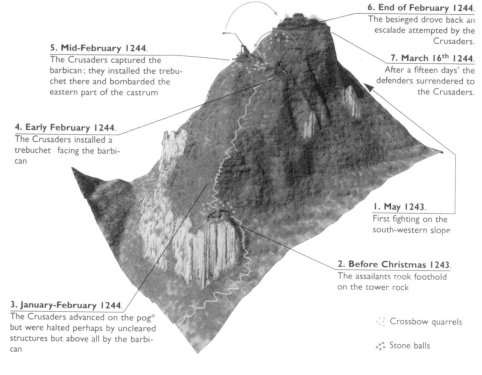

6. End of February 1244.
The besieged drove back an escalade attempted by the Crusaders.

7. March 16ᵗʰ 1244.
After a fifteen days' the defenders surrendered to the Crusaders.

5. Mid-February 1244.
The Crusaders captured the barbican; they installed the trebuchet there and bombarded the eastern part of the castrum

4. Early February 1244.
The Crusaders installed a trebuchet facing the barbican

1. May 1243.
First fighting on the south-western slope

2. Before Christmas 1243.
The assailants took foothold on the tower rock

3. January-February 1244.
The Crusaders advanced on the pog* but were halted perhaps by uncleared structures but above all by the barbican

Crossbow quarrels

Stone balls

The siege of Montsegur

an object of great religious and esoteric significance; perhaps the Holy Chalice itself, brought to France by Mary Magdalene and Joseph of Arimathea; perhaps plunder hidden in the mountains of the Razès and Sabarthès when the great Visigoth Empire fell in the 5th century; perhaps the riches of Dagobert II, the last of the great Merovingian kings who preceded the dynasty of Charles the Hammer and Charlemagne.

A few days before Christmas, two Cathars, a deacon and a *parfait* clambered down from the *castrum*. By chance, they came across Crusader sentries that they vaguely knew who let them pass and showed them a safe path through the siege. From Montségur, the two men made their way to the county of Foix and hid the precious consignment of coins, jewellery and, perhaps, ingots of gold and silver in a *spoulga* – a fortified cave. The *spoulga* was commanded by Pierre-Roger of Mirepoix's brother-in-law, Arnaud, a devoted Cathar believer.

Despite this success, as the weather turned colder, confidence was ebbing away from the 'safe mountain'. The inquisitor was later told:

*W*hen Bernard of Carcassonne, one of the *sergents* of Montségur, was mortally wounded, he was consoled in the house of the bishop of the heretics, Bertrand Marty. I was there with several other people, but I can't remember who because we were all running this way and that because of the constant attacks.

In the mayhem, the defenders feared dying without receiving the *consolamentum*. Without it they would fail to 'make a good end' and their soul would be forced within to migrate to a new body. To avoid this, they entered into a *convenenza* – agreement in *langue d'oc* – as explained by Philippa of Péreille, sister of Raymond of Péreille, lord of Montségur, and wife of Pierre-Roger of Mirepoix, leader of the garrison:

'*A*nd so, all together, we asked the Bishop Bertrand Marty and the other *parfaits*, should we be mortally wounded and unconscious, that they should receive us and console us even if we could no longer speak. They promised.'

CHAPTER 48

The Fall of Montségur

t Christmas, the attackers took the barbican. Now they were within only a few dozen yards of the fortress. It was still inaccessible – in that the attackers would have had to make their way along a ridge less than 6 feet wide with a sheer drop on either side – but it allowed them to install a new siege gun. The southern and eastern walls of the citadel were easy targets.

Pierre-Roger of Mirepoix realised that, without assistance from Raymond VII of Toulouse, it was only a matter of time before the fortress fell. In the valley below, the standards and banners of the Catholic church and the *fleur-de-lys* of the French king – tattered and faded now after ten months of first heat, then rain, then snow – were still flying. The Crusader army numbered between 6,000 and 10,000. Inside were no more than a hundred fighting men.

In the new year of 1244, twenty-five fighting men were sent from the nearby *château* of Usson to reinforce the *pog*. Another man, an expert in siege weaponry, slipped through the siege. He claimed to have been sent by Raymond VII who was determined to come to their aid soon. A letter came for Bertrand Marty from the Cathar bishop of Cremona in northern Italy, asking him to send two *parfaits* to support the work of his church, which 'lived in peace'.

In mid-February, the attackers pushed forward yet again. An attempt with scaling ladders on the walls of the *castrum* itself was only just repelled. Losses became heavy among the defenders and more and more entered into a *convenenza*. Mathieu, one of the two Cathars who smuggled away the 'treasure', also returned to Montségur in the third week of February. Again he slipped through the blockade with the complicity of local Crusader sentries. He reported that the money was safe and brought with him two crossbowmen and two *sergents*. Mathieu told the leaders of the garrison to hold on until Easter 'because the count of Toulouse will be returning to Languedoc with mighty reinforcements'. Perhaps in the spring, once the mountain passes reopened, there might even be troops sent by the king of Aragon. In reality, time was running out.

On 1 March 1244, a final desperate attempt was made to dislodge the Basques from the Roc de la Tour. The next day, Pierre-Roger of Mirepoix discussed the situation with Bertrand Marty. They decided that, clearly, Raymond of Toulouse would not come. Pierre-Roger commanded a single horn to be sounded on the ramparts of the ravaged stronghold. Then he and Raymond of Péreille walked down the battle-scarred mountainside and surrendered to Hugues des Arcis, the royal governor of Carcassonne, and Peter Amiel, archbishop of Narbonne.

Winter had been harsh. Both sides were exhausted, negotiations were short and the terms offered generous, as if neither side had any more strength to fight. The act of surrender was signed the same day, on 2 March 1244. Nine months after the banners of the Catholic church and the crown of France had first fluttered bright in the valley below the mountain, Montségur had fallen.

The act of surrender required hostages to be given. (They included Bertrand Marty's brother Raymond, the old knight Arnald-Roger of Mirepoix and Raymond of Péreille's young son, Jordan.) Also, Montségur must become the property of the Catholic church and the French crown. The 400 or so inhabitants would be pardoned for their past crimes, even including the massacre of Guillaume Arnaut's inquisitorial team at Avignonet. The fighting men would be set free with only light penances, once they had been confessed to the inquisitorial registers. All who abjured their 'heretical' beliefs would also be allowed to walk free, punished only by the obligation to wear a cross on their clothes. Any who would not recant the Cathar faith would be burnt at the stake.

The interrogations were undertaken by the inquisitor Ferrer, between 10 March and 27 May 1244. Eighteen statements have survived, thanks in large part to a set of copies drawn up by Colbert in the 17th century. (Over the years, many inquisitorial registers – including Ferrer's – were lost, especially during the French Revolution.)

The act of surrender also included a two-week truce. Why? What needed to be done that had not already been done? The 'treasure' was safe, the surrender settlement was acceptable. Easter fell within the period of ceasefire – was that it? Or were there other secrets to be concealed, other rites to accomplish? Was it the spring equinox? What was so important as to make the Cathars stay in that cold and damaged mountain fortress a little longer, after all they had already suffered?

The mangonels, catapults and other siege engines fell silent. Inside the fortress, life fell into a new and peaceful rhythm, unknown for nine months. The surviving *parfaits* fasted, as usual. Those who were preparing to die took leave of their families and friends. The inquisitional register lists the objects given by the *parfaits* to their protectors, touchingly reminiscent of gifts they might have given in the golden age of the Cathar church – cloth, wax, wool, clothing. Pierre-Roger of Mirepoix received a blanket full of money, gifts from believers, and '400 *sous toulzas*' – coins from Toulouse – to share among his men 'as wages or as gifts'. For the same purpose, Bertrand Marty gave him oil, salt, pepper, wax and a piece of green cloth. Other Cathars gave food and fifty jerkins. A *parfait* presented one of the *sergents* with a wagonload of wheat. The *parfaite* Marquésia gave all her belongings to her granddaughter Philippa, Pierre-Roger's wife. Others gave shoes, a purse, breeches. Someone gave a felt hat.

Before the ceasefire ended, on Sunday 13 March, when only a few days of freedom remained, twenty-one ordinary believers – including women, knights and men-at-arms – asked to be given the *consolament* and received fully into the Cathar church. In doing this, they volunteered their bodies to the flames of the inquisitors' pyre and their souls to God. Not a single one of the *parfaits* abjured.

Some 300 metres below in the valley, Hugues des Arcis supervised the construction of a wooden palisade on the southwestern face of the mountain. His men gathered wood from the forests and dismantled some of the last bedraggled huts of the decimated *castrum* of Montségur for firewood. They collected straw and faggots, soaking them in pitch to help the damp timber to catch. Ladders were propped outside the pen. Inside was a spine of wooden stakes to which the 'heretics' would be tied. The inquisitors hung back from these preparations – the judicial murders would be carried out by the 'secular arm'.

Once the pyre was ready, the Cathars would be burnt alive en masse. Some say, on the following evening, four *parfaits* slipped away carrying the church's holy books – rites, rituals and other illicit texts in Occitan. Others maintain that it was on 15 March 1244, the eve of the final conquest of the *castrum*, that four *parfaits* were lowered with ropes down the steepest precipice. They slipped away through the incomplete blockade and headed for the *spoulga* where, in December, the 'treasure' was hidden. They met Mathieu, collected the hoard and went on to the *château* of Usson. The 'treasure' was again made safe.

Then two of the four *parfaits* set off for Italy, carrying news of the devastating defeat to the bishop of Cremona.

▦ CHAPTER 49 ▦

Death at Montségur

t dawn on Wednesday, 16 March 1244, Hugues des Arcis, royal governor of Carcassonne, took possession of Montségur in the name of the king of France. The archbishop of Narbonne, Peter Amiel, collected together at least 220 *parfaits*, *parfaites* and newly consoled believers. Among the converts were Raymond of Péreille's wife, Corba, and his daughter, Philippa, wife of Pierre-Roger of Mirepoix. There were also four knights, four unmarried soldiers and two with their wives, two messengers, a squire, a crossbowman and a merchant. Not one would recant their faith.

The Cathars left the *castrum* in shackles. At their head was Bertrand Marty, an old man, barefoot, dressed in coarse, dark robes. The soldiers half led and half dragged them down the couple of hundred yards of steeply sloping mountainside. One by one, clumsy in their chains, they climbed the ladders propped against the wooden walls and jumped down into the pyre to be tethered like animals to the stakes. Around them on the mountain, there were still patches of snow on the ground.

Burning faggots were thrown in at each of the four corners of the enclosure. The men of God – Catholic priests, bishops, monks, the inquisitors Ferrer and Duranti – began to chant psalms celebrating God's mercy and goodness. The rough hems of the Cathars' robes caught alight. Perhaps, in part, the psalms covered the sounds of the voices of the dying, the crackling of the straw and the hissing of human fat. Almost gleefully, the Catholic chronicler Guillaume of Puylaurens wrote: 'Refusing the conversion to which they were exhorted, they were burnt in an enclosure made of sticks and stakes which was set on fire and despatched them to the fire of Tartarus.'

Even today, there is a spirit of place at Montségur that reveals that something terrible once happened there. It is a 'haunted mountain', as the great Occitan poet and historian René Nelli once called it.

More than 700 years later, in 1960, a small stone memorial was erected on the approximate site of the mass execution, an acre or two of land known as the *prat dels cremats* – the field of the burned. Like the dove of light at Minerve, the memorial is inscribed '*Als Catars*' – 'To the Cathars'. Winter or spring, there are always small tributes laid at its foot, flowers, scraps of poetry, ribbons.

CHAPTER 50

The End

After the fall of Montségur in 1244, the village and fortifications on top of the *pog* were utterly destroyed. The land and foundations were given to an old companion of Simon of Montfort, Guy of Lévis. In the mountains and on the plains, the Crusader army continued its work, mopping up pockets of resistance. The Inquisition, too, pursued its ignoble office, punishing, condemning, imprisoning and burning.

Pons Viguier, a Cathar believer imprisoned in the *château* Narbonnais in Toulouse in June 1246, tried to disassociate himself from the horror: 'My wife has just left me, this month, and I think she has become a heretic. But I don't know where she is, I haven't seen her since.'

Around the same time, an informer told the pitiful story of two *parfaites*:

One day when my son Arnaud was ill and Doctor John was attending him in my house, Guilhem Faure, the bailiff of Saint-Martin, came in with two heretic women. One of them had a broken arm. Guilhem Faure asked the doctor to treat her; he refused. Guilhem Faure left the house with the two heretic women and, the next day, they were arrested and burnt.

Two years after the fall of Montségur, Louis IX of France conducted negotiations with Raymond Trencavel, officially relieving him of all his feudal rights in Languedoc. Trencavel committed to accompanying Louis on an eastern Crusade and he and the renowned *faydit* Olivier of Termes travelled together on the king's ship. On their return, Louis IX gave Trencavel land.

At Montségur, Raymond VII of Toulouse had failed to come to the rescue of his people. Worse, in order to try to regain the approval of the Catholic church,

The lices *in Carcassonne today.*

Raymond decided he would have to make good on his repeated promise to eradicate the 'heretics'. He made a pilgrimage to Compostela and eighty Cathars were burnt on his orders at Agen. In 1247, he was rewarded with the return of his title of duke of Narbonne. His daughter, Jeanne, left for the Holy Land with her husband, Alphonse of Poitiers, younger brother of the French king.

Also in 1247, Carcassonne submitted formally to the rule of King Louis IX of France – later Saint-Louis. Louis founded the *bastide*, a new Carcassonne on the flat land on the west bank of the Aude. He and his successor, Philip III, built the second outer ring of ramparts round the Cité, enclosing a wide flat area of *lices* – lists. According to contemporary chronicles, the fortress was impregnable once more.

In September 1249, Raymond VII died and Alphonse of Poitiers became count of Toulouse.

Even after Montségur fell, a few isolated refuges remained, perched high up in the Corbières. At Puilaurens the entrance to the *château* was protected by a chicane of parallel walls designed as a killing ground for infantry attack. A channel has been cut in the internal wall of one of the towers as a way of making the defenders' voices carry from top to bottom or from bottom to top. According to legend, this is the *tour de la Dame Blanche* – the White Lady's tower – supposedly named for a 14th-century niece of King Philippe le Bel of France, whose pale ghost walks the night-time battlements draped in ghastly muslin. Puilaurens was finally taken around 1250.

The last to fall was Quéribus, another extraordinary fortress that seems to grow organically out of the tortured limestone of the landscape, 730 metres above sea level.

On a clear day, the inhabitants could see all the way to the massive Canigou mountain at Perpignan on the Mediterranean and, looking northwest, signallers could send messages to Peyrepertuse. The main entrance was protected by a bottleneck in the path up the mountainside. The walls of the keep were so thick that, within them, the builders concealed a secret room that led into a tunnel, giving access to an outpost – now ruined – on the cliffside.

Queribus – one of the cinq fils *of Carcassonne*

The French army finally arrived at Quéribus in 1255. As they made their way along the twisted valley roads between the peaks, the defenders – including the veteran Chabert of Barbaira – slipped away without a fight, probably to Aragon in Spain or to Piedmont in what is now northern Italy. The force that finally took Quéribus was led by Olivier of Termes.

Son of Raymond of Termes, nephew of Benoît the Cathar bishop, Olivier was born with the century. At just ten years old, he was eyewitness to the brutality of Montfort's Crusade when his home at Termes was overrun by siege. Throughout the long, grinding extermination of the Cathars, Olivier the *faydit* remained a devoted ally of the itinerant *parfaits* and their persecuted flock. He shared part of his friend Roger Trencavel's exile in Aragon and enthusiastically joined the rebellion in 1240. The rebellion's failure, despite popular support, dented his confidence. After the fall of Montségur, he lost heart completely, entering the service of the French king.

Olivier of Termes was rewarded with the restitution of his family's lands and pursued a long career as a Crusader in North Africa and the Holy Land, where he died in 1274. Some historians – perhaps those with a really well-developed sense of irony – say his body is buried at Fontfroide, the home of Peter of Castelnau.

Meanwhile, in England, Amaury of Montfort's brother, Simon the Younger, finally became 6th earl of Leicester, the title their father had never been allowed to inherit. Simon the Younger later took on the role of leader of the baronial opposition to King Henry III of England. After the English rebellion of 1263–4, the Frenchman Simon of Montfort and Leicester became *de facto* ruler of England and called Europe's first directly elected parliament since the time of ancient Athens.

In the east, the Crusader state of Antioch fell in 1268. Two years later, Louis IX led the Eighth Crusade, accompanied by the future Edward I of England. It, too, was a military failure, diverted from its original goal of aiding the Crusader states to a plague-wracked siege of Tunis, where Louis himself succumbed. So did Roger, 'son of Trencavel, so-called viscount of Béziers' – the end of the line.

A version of the ancient arms of the Montfort family.

The following year, Alphonse of Poitiers died and all the domains of Toulouse reverted to the French crown. The inquisitor Jean Galand continued his investigations in Languedoc, including a Montagne Noire stronghold Montfort had originally not dared to attack – Cabaret. The place had been a possession of the French royal family since 1229. Even then, something of the spirit of the place must have endured. Galand found evidence that, as late as 1273 and 1284, the royally appointed owners of the castle died consoled in the Cathar faith. But the true Cabaret of *paratge* was gone.

In 1276, in northern Italy, the Inquisition rounded up 200 Cathars, including several Italian bishops and a large number of refugees from Languedoc. Two years later, they were all burnt in the Roman arena in Verona.

The Catholic church also imposed itself in architecture. Begun in 1282, the cathedral of Sainte-Cecelia in Albi, for example, has no glorious western façade, facing the evening sun. It has no high welcoming porch. It was designed to dominate the town where Bernard of Clairvaux was mocked by Cathars in 1145. It is one of Europe's largest brick-built structures and resembles nothing so much as a fortress, grim and forbidding, a symbol of the Catholic triumph over the Cathar 'heresy' of universal salvation – the Albigensian Crusade.

The cathedral was not finished until the end of the 15th-century

Towards the end of the 13th century, the Inquisition was also building its own prisons in Carcassonne, Toulouse, Albi and Pamiers, usually called *Murs* – walls. There were two grades of imprisonment. Under a regime of *murus largus*, the prisoner could remain in contact with the outside world, including visits home in the case of family illness or, for women, to give birth. In *murus strictus*, the prisoner was enclosed in solitary confinement on a diet of bread and water, in irons or chained to the wall of a small dark cell.

The consuls of Carcassonne sent a letter of complaint to the inquisitor Jean Galand in 1285:

*Y*ou have had built a prison you call the Mur but which would be better named Hell itself. There are little rooms where you mistreat and torture people. They defecate and urinate where they stand and have no choice but to sleep on the cold ground. They are held in these conditions, night and day, for long periods.

Sometimes imprisonment was justified as a means of bringing about repentance. But the extremity of the inquisitors' behaviour provoked popular revolts in Albi, Limoux and Carcassonne. The French king was obliged to come south to Toulouse then Carcassonne. In 1305, the disturbances came to an end when forty bourgeois were hanged in Limoux and fifteen in the Cité.

Also around the turn of the century, Guy of Lévis's family built a castle on the site of the ruined *castrum* of Montségur. It is this castle that tourists visit today – the Cathar *castrum* is long gone. Some suggest that the ruined fortress on top of the *pog* is a solar temple or a shrine to gnostic revelation, or look for the special alignments of the windows and arrow-slits or come on particular days or nights of the year, hoping to discover some unusual geometry of sunlight or moonlight and stone. It is possible, of course, that the *château* at Montségur is a temple of some kind, but it isn't a Cathar temple.

Meanwhile, despite all the defeats and all the punishments, in a nearby Pyrenean valley, the religion of the *Bons Chrétiens* was on the cusp of an extraordinary and unlikely renaissance.

⚎ CHAPTER 51 ⚎

The Last Cathars in Languedoc

Though Olivier of Termes had completely lost heart, many had not. Faith was still faith. In both Aragon in Spain and in northern Italy, Cathar beliefs were still common. In both regions, Occitan – or a dialect very close to it – could be spoken. A Languedoc 'church in exile' had been developing in Lombardy from the first dreadful years of inquisitional persecution.

Pierre Authié was a notary from the Pyrenean spa town of Ax-les-Thermes. In 1296, he was fifty years old, extremely wealthy and the possessor of a substantial library that included books of Cathar ritual and theology. He and his brother, Guillaume, decided to travel to Italy in order to be consoled and ordained as *parfaits*.

The voyage was complex and the preparation for ordination time-consuming. They returned home in 1300 with three other Languedoc *Bons Chrétiens*, all of whom were ordained in Italy. They visited a money-changer in Toulouse, then climbed back up the valley of the Ariège to Ax. For a while they hid in another brother's cellar, but they were spotted by an informer, who was only prevented from denouncing them to the Inquisition when friends of the Authié family 'made him disappear' in the mountains.

They began preaching, travelling on foot from village to village just as their predecessors had done. The group was joined by a sixth *parfait*. Pierre ordained his son, Jacques, and two other men. In 1301, they were all together in Ax and then Limoux. Another convert, Philippe d'Alayrac, was sent to Sicily to be ordained by a venerable Cathar *parfait* in exile there. When he returned, he was accompanied by the woman *parfaite* Aude Bourrel.

Though their evangelism began with well-off professionals, many common people were moved to convert or reassert their faith. In 1302, Pierre

Authié consoled Roger-Bernard, count of Foix, on his death bed. But the success of their ministry still depended on slipping through the tightening net of inquisitional persecution.

In 1305, two of the group were denounced and captured. They escaped from the prison of the Mur at Carcassonne, but terror gripped their people. Ten converts from Arques fled to Lyon to confess their 'heresy' to Pope Clement V and ask for pardon. Many villages were investigated. Informers were found who were willing to point out believers for the inquisitors to punish. Still, at the end of 1306, Pierre Authié ordained two more *parfaits*.

In January of the following year, the Dominican Bernard Gui joined the Toulouse Inquisition. As the Authié group continued their remarkable ministry in the hills, Gui reinvigorated the Catholics' mopping-up operation. In 1307, Aude Bourrel, the last known Languedoc *parfaite*, died of natural causes after living for several years in the rue de l'Etoile in Toulouse with a Cathar believer named Esclarmonde. At Easter 1308, Gui announced three burnings and two exhumations, read out with great pomp from the highest step of the cathedral of Saint-Etienne in a pale replica of the Last Judgment. Philippe d'Alayrac was arrested but escaped with Guilhem Bélibaste, the man who would become the last *Bon Chrétien* in Languedoc.

Bélibaste came from a well-off family of Languedoc peasant farmers, all of whom were Cathar believers. Shortly after the turn of the century, Bélibaste killed a shepherd who threatened to denounce his family to the Inquisition and went into hiding with

Bernard Gui, a particularly severe 14th-century inquisitor, brought all the practices of investigation together in his manual Practica Inquisitionis. He is the inquisitor who appears – not entirely authentically – in Umberto Eco's The Name of the Rose. This is a page from the register of his colleague, Bernard of Caux.

Authié's *parfaits*. Arrested with Philippe d'Alayrac, he escaped and fled into Aragon and became well known to small communities of refugees from the French Pyrenees.

In May 1309, Gui announced ninety-one condemnations, including fifty *murus strictus* and six exhumations, including Aude Bourrel. In August, he made it known that Pierre Authié was a wanted man.

On 8 September 1309, the Pyrenean village of Montaillou was surrounded by a troupe of armed men, a hundred years after Catholic monks first turned their suspicious eyes on it. The inhabitants were imprisoned in the nearby *château* by the jailer of the Carcassonne Mur. Meanwhile, the inquisitor set up his interrogation rooms in the home of the local Catholic priest, Pierre Clergue, himself a Cathar sympathiser.

Pierre Authié was arrested and brought to the Mur prison in Toulouse. One of his group, Amiel of Perles, was already there, an old man in declining health. Amiel went on a hunger strike and, on 23 October, Gui had him quickly burnt to prevent him 'escaping the flames'.

In April 1310, Pierre Authié listened to Gui deliver another 113 condemnations, including six exhumations and seventeen death sentences. The 'secular arm' built a pyre in front of the cathedral of Saint-Etienne and Pierre and the others were burnt. Pierre's brother and son and another *parfait* of their group suffered the same fate in Carcassonne. Philippe d'Alayrac had by now ordained Bélibaste – who scraped a living as a maker of combs – as they fled from town to town, but was taken and burnt in the same year. Barely a single member of the unlikely Cathar renaissance was left.

In April 1312, Gui sentenced another 225 people. In Spain, Bélibaste took up residence in Morella near to a small community of refugees from Montaillou, including the shepherd Pierre Maury. In order to deflect suspicion, he set up home as a married man with his mistress, Raymonde. In 1314, he met Raymond of Castelnau, a *parfait* from Agen. Raymond of Castelnau died two years later and Bélibaste, a lapsed *parfait* who lived in sin, against his vows, with a mistress, attended his funeral. Castelnau was the second-to-last ordained minister of the Cathar church in Languedoc or Aragon. Should Bélibaste take it into his head to mend his ways, there was no one left to renew his vows.

In 1319, Raymonde became pregnant and, for appearance's sake, Bélibaste asked her to marry Pierre Maury, but he soon regretted it and Raymonde returned to live with him. Not long after, a man called Arnaud Sicre came to live among the refugees from Montaillou. His mother had refused to abjure Catharism and had been burnt, making Sicre an ideal double agent for the Inquisition.

Sicre claimed to have known the Authié brothers and used the family of Pierre Maury, the shepherd, to gain an introduction to Bélibaste. He managed to get Bélibaste to admit that he pretended to give a Catholic blessing to the corpse of Raymond of Castelnau and took careful note of the Cathar's ritual prayers for which he woke six times each night.

Sicre returned to Languedoc to make an interim report to his inquisitorial masters. He told the refugees that he was going to visit an old rich aunt and her pretty daughter, hoping to persuade them to come and join the community in Aragon. He returned a little before Christmas 1320 with money he said was a gift from his aunt to help the community celebrate. In fact, it was given to him by the inquisitor Jacques Fournier, who had taken over the investigations at Montaillou.

The inquisitor Jacques Fournier collected statements from 95 of the 200-odd inhabitants of Montaillou, some of which took several days to complete. The register of Fournier's investigation formed the basis for Emmanuel Leroy Ladurie's brilliant reconstruction Montaillou: Village Occitan. *Fournier is seen here in his later role as Pope Benedict XII.*

Arnaud Sicre told the Cathars that illness prevented his aunt from making the voyage and that the pretty niece was obliged to stay at her side. Sicre's aunt would be pleased, however, to receive the visit of a *Bon Chrétien*.

At Easter 1321, Sicre, Bélibaste and Pierre and Arnaud Maury set off for Languedoc. Bélibaste and the Maurys tried to get Sicre drunk to test his story, but he held firm. The four were arrested, of course, and Bélibaste never consoled the fictional aunt on her death bed. Sicre asked that the two Maurys should be released and he and Bélibaste were imprisoned together by the Inquisition, to hide, for the time being, Sicre's treachery. Bélibaste told Sicre that he had harboured suspicions of him from the first because of his imperfect *melhorament* – his ritual Cathar greeting and request for God's blessing.

The two men were held in chains together in a room at the top of a tower in Castelbon in the county of Foix. Bélibaste told Sicre:

*W*ere you able to mend your ways and repent for what you have done to me, I would console you and we could throw ourselves off this tower together. Immediately our souls would ascend to Heaven to be with our Heavenly Father...I care nothing for my flesh for nothing in it is truly mine. It belongs to the worms. And there is nothing of the Holy Father in my flesh and he doesn't wish it in his kingdom, because the flesh of men belongs to he who made it, the Prince of this material world, and the Heavenly Father wants nothing that was made by the god and Prince of this material world.

Bélibaste spoke well and with dignity. Sicre was frightened that the Cathar might attempt to force suicide on him and was grateful for their chains. All the same, Bélibaste knew well that, in reality, he no longer possessed the 'power to save souls'; his vows were in tatters and he was alone.

Bélibaste was brought to Carcassonne in 1321 for interrogation, then burnt at Villerouge-Termenès, the last known Cathar in Languedoc. Sicre was released and granted a reward. It included the house and property of his mother, seized by the Catholic church when she died the same horrific death for the faith her son betrayed.

CHAPTER 52

The Last Templars

In her brilliant book *Femmes Cathares*, Anne Brenon says:

> The female Cathar believer was, quite simply, a medieval Christian woman with no desire, indeed no reason to curse God for the horrors of the world, for the triumph of injustice and stupidity, for the death of a child…and who saw her church's priests not as special, privileged beings, but as guides to the way.

But without priests with the power to save souls, the Cathar church was destroyed. All that was left was to pursue and convert or punish the remaining congregation. In 1328, for example, the inquisitor of Montaillou, Jacques Fournier, walled up 500 believers in the caves of Lombrives.

The destruction of the Cathar church in Languedoc was accompanied by the destruction of the feudal order. The lands of Toulouse and Trencavel were absorbed by the French crown. At the beginning of the 14th century, France and the Catholic church turned their attention to another group whose wealth and influence they coveted: the Knights Templar.

Between their foundation in the early 12th century and their extermination at the beginning of the 14th, the Templars spread throughout France. Their dates run parallel to those of the Cathars of Languedoc and elsewhere, but there are almost no points of historical contact between the two groups. Templars and Cathars are associated in people's minds because of this bland historical coincidence of dates, and because they were both persecuted and annihilated by the same oppressors – an alliance of territorial ambition and dogmatic doctrinal certitude.

The pope at that time was a Frenchman, Clement V, a weak leader who Philip the Fair of France persuaded to join his own party. This was important because it would allow Philip to get hold of Templar possessions overseas as well as in France – the agreement of the pope extended Philip's jurisdiction to the Holy Land.

Revelations were leaked of the alleged foul and 'heretical' practices of the Knights Templar in their secret ceremonies, including perversions of baptism and mass, spitting on the cross, denying Christ, sodomy, idolatry, kissing one another's anus and the worship of cats and other witch familiars. Secret orders were sent out throughout France and every Templar who could be found was arrested on a single day, 13 October 1307. Philip's counsellors claimed the arrests were made with the support of Catholic inquisitors but they were unaware of the action. Many Templars were tortured in order to obtain confessions. Many gave in. Many confessed rather than face torture. Their last grand master, Jacques de Molay, later admitted that he had lied to save his life.

Pope Clement V changed his mind and protested. Philip had bestowed on himself the title of 'champion and defender of the faith'. A show trial was organised at which a large number of Templar members publicly 'confessed'. Clement insisted that authority for the continuing investigation should return to the Catholic church and that it should range over Templar activities in Europe and the Holy Land. The investigation was undertaken by local bishops and monastic inquisitors. Almost everywhere – in Portugal, Spain, Germany, Cyprus and Italy – the Templars were found innocent. But in France there was no further investigation and the inquisitors merely concentrated on urging the 'guilty' to repent.

Despite the supposed 'guilt' of the individuals, the order itself hadn't been condemned. The debate rumbled on and no evidence of any departure from the original 'rule' drawn up with the assistance of Bernard of Clairvaux could be proved. The pope hesitated, then decided by Apostolic Decree – the papal bull of 22 March 1312 – that the order should finally be suppressed. Its property was given over to the Hospitallers to be used in the failing defence of the Crusader states of the Holy Land. In Portugal, where Templar guilt was strongly disputed, the new Order of Christ in Portugal was endowed with Templar property. In Aragon in Spain, the Order of Montesa inherited.

Any Templar found not guilty was free to join these or other orders or relinquish monastic orders and return to secular life. Templars judged guilty were – in the time-honoured expression of the inquisitors – 'handed over to the secular arm' for punishment. The sentence was said, by the Catholic church, to treat them 'according to the rigours of justice, tempered by a generous mercy'.

In March 1314, Jacques de Molay, the last Templar grand master, was brought to a platform in front of the cathedral church of Notre-Dame in Paris in order that he might publicly admit his 'guilt' one last time. The Inquisition had developed a routine of declamation of sentences from the steps of great churches and this reading was supposed to open the event. Molay was accompanied by three Templar lieutenants who were supposed to follow his lead. But Molay's courage returned and he declared to the assembled crowd that he was innocent and ready to die. One of Molay's companions joined him in proclaiming his innocence.

The burning of Jacques of Molay

It must have been a moment of extraordinary public drama. The crowd, we are told, were enormously impressed by the elderly grand master. It is often said that, as the flames rose, he laid a curse on the persecutors of the Temple. What is certain is that, within the year, Philip the Fair, king of France, Nogaret, his lord chancellor, and Pope Clement V were dead.

🔲 CHAPTER 53 🔲

The Fall and Rise and
Fall of Carcassonne

he Templars were gone; the Cathars too. In 1355, the army of
Edward, the Black Prince, destroyed the Carcassonne *bastide* – the
low town on the far bank of the Aude first built by Louis IX – but
failed to take the Cité on the Hill. As the years passed, however,
Carcassonne became sidelined as military conflict edged further and further
away from the fortress.

Finally, in 1659, over 1,000
years of cross-Pyrenean conflict
were more or less ended when
France and Spain signed the
Treaty of the Pyrenees. The
French evacuated their last forts
in Aragon and took possession
of all the towns and villages
north and east of the Pyrenees.
The crests of the mountain chain
became the border between the
two countries and the fortified
Cité of Carcassonne and the
Pyrenean frontier forts known
by tourism as the *châteaux
Cathares* were made obsolete.

Haphazard shanty buildings in the lices *–
'lists' – between the two rings of city walls.*

The upkeep of the forti-fications of Carcassonne was abandoned. Like any garrison town, this brought on an economic crisis. If the Cité was to enjoy prosperity, it would have to reinvent itself as an economic centre – as it had once been before the Crusade against the Cathars, Trencavel's bustling capital. It still had the advantage of its location – the Carcassonne gap between the Montagne Noire and the Corbières, channelling people and goods north and south between the Atlantic and the Mediterranean. There was trade with the upper valley of the Aude and Ariège.

Nevertheless, the upkeep of the region's roads was expensive. They were, of course, unmetalled and easily damaged by heavy carts laden with wheat, timber and other commodities. But what alternative was there? Few of the region's natural waterways were navigable – too shallow in summer and autumn, unpredictable torrents in winter and spring. Engineering techniques for managing their flow were undeveloped. A solution was found that had first been suggested during the Roman occupation of Languedoc. It was decided to attempt the building of a canal.

There was – and is – a watershed just south of Toulouse where the rivers have to decide whether to flow north to Bordeaux or south to Narbonne. Perhaps there could be a reservoir at this point, constantly replenished with melting snow, feeding an artificial waterway whose surface needed no maintenance, along whose length a single horse could pull extraordinarily heavy loads.

In 1636, a committee had studied the question. One of the members of the committee was Pierre-Paul Riquet, baron of Bonrepos, a twenty-seven-year-old engineer from Béziers. He observed the course of streams washing down from the Montagne Noire, looking for the *ligne de partage des eaux* – the place of the sharing of the waters. He identified the watershed at a place called the *seuil* –

It was Louis XIV who instructed architects to massively extend and embellish the modest palace of Versailles and move the monarchy and government out of Paris – and out of reach of the mob. Louis also paid for the building of the Pont Royal from his own pocket and, among many other projects, financed construction of the Champs-Elysées, the place Vendôme and the place des Victoires, which was created to commemorate the triumph over the Spanish. His projects extended to many regional French towns and cities and, late in his reign in 1702, he had street lighting installed in the streets of the capital, founded the police force and divided the city into twenty *quartiers* – we now call the twenty divisions *arrondissements*.

the 'threshold' – of Naurouze and chose this point as the centre of his canal, from which water would gradually flow down through locks into the Atlantic Ocean and the Mediterranean Sea. The location was fully 48 metres above the level of the nearest major river, the Garonne.

Construction of the Canal du Midi began in 1666, the year of the Great Fire of London. Louis XIV, the Sun King, was on the throne of France, an admirer of grand building projects. The king would contribute 40 per cent, the regional coffers 40 per cent and Riquet would provide the final 20 per cent. Once built, Riquet himself would be the canal's owner. The 241-kilometre canal took fifteen years to build and employed more than 12,000 workers. Riquet died in 1680 in Toulouse, without ever seeing it in service. Work was completed by his two sons and the first traffic embarked in 1681, just one year later.

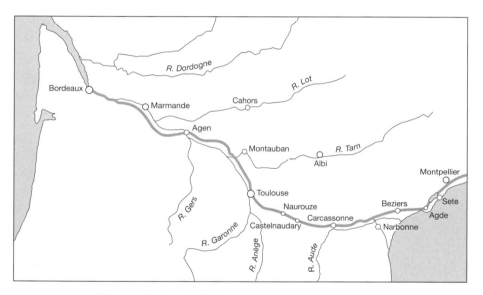

The route of the canal joining the Atlantic and Mediterranean.

Despite the economic impetus given by the canal, the region's economy did not flourish as anticipated. Despite moving the frontier, continuing conflict with Spain and others pushed the French state's finances deeply into the red, increasing the tax burden – not on the church or the nobility, who paid virtually no taxes whatsoever, but on the middle and working classes.

In France, the Sun King still reigned in splendour by divine right. Those same middle- and working-class people cannot have failed to notice that in

1649, across the English Channel, a king had been executed and a civil government put in his place. Then, in 1688, the Glorious Revolution in England replaced the despised Catholic James II with his Protestant daughter, Mary, and her husband, William of Orange, who ruled together as constitutional monarchs.

In Carcassonne, the people had begun successfully to develop the local economy. By the early 18th century it was known as 'the manufacturing centre of Languedoc'. Here and there the roads were improving. (The Scot John Loudon McAdam, who developed the techniques that would lead to impermeable road surfaces made of tarmac, was born in 1756.) Nationally, however, the fractures in society were having a depressing impact on economic growth. In 1776, the French became intellectually and emotionally engaged in the American War of Independence, most notably through the Marquis de Lafayette, who fought extensively on the American side against the forces of the English king. It seemed that, on the far side of the Atlantic, a bright new dawn was possible. Why not at home? Louis XIV's successors Louis XV and XVI were aware that they had to respond to the unrest, but their strategies were too feeble and too piecemeal to prevent the catastrophe that awaited them and the French monarchy.

Finally, in 1788, the accident of poor weather and – therefore – a poor harvest led to a period of punishing inflation, price speculation and hoarding of commodities. It set a lighted taper to the powder keg of discontent. In May 1789, the king called a great council of state – the Etats Généraux – to calm the situation, but it merely served to make more widely known the desperate condition of the public purse. The council was renamed the Assemblée Nationale, the forerunner of the French democratic parliament.

On 14 July 1789, anger had reached a peak in the capital. The mob sought a symbolic target for its rage. At the prison of the Bastille just seven prisoners were held, but it also contained a large stock of gunpowder belonging to the royalist forces. The building was attacked and the French Revolution had crossed its Rubicon. The entire prison was dismantled stone by stone and fragments dispersed throughout France.

For several years the Revolutionary government proceeded to dismantle what they called the 'neo-feudal' structures of French society. They sought to liberate the nation from a straitjacket of oppressive corporate controls and release free, responsible individuals from the tyranny of the past. But destruction came at considerable cost and some aspects of the old regime that had functioned for the benefit of the people – such as church alms for the poor, hospitals and education – were lost.

The response of the Revolutionary authorities under Robespierre was the Terror. In 1793–4, more than 16,000 people were executed. The slightest suspicion, the least-tenable denunciation, could lead to the scaffold. Half a million French men and women were imprisoned and more than a quarter of a million placed under house arrest. Judicial murder extended to both radical and moderate members of government and Robespierre's autocratic dictatorship lost public support. In response, a new constitution was drawn up and, for the first time, France was governed by 750 representatives in twin chambers of parliament.

But the experiment was short-lived. Ten years on from the Storming of the Bastille, the Revolution did not seem to have achieved enough. On 9 November 1799, Napoleon Bonaparte, defender of the Revolution and the nation's most successful general, announced: 'Citizens, the Revolution has been established according to the principles which inspired it. It is over.'

Napoleon was to become emperor. He was, first and last, a soldier. When asked for advice on how to deal with the pope, he recommended imagining the pontiff had an army of 200,000 men. When he died, in 1821, it was with the words 'Tête d'armée' – Head of the army – on his lips. Yet he ordered that the ancient fortress of Carcassonne should be struck from the roster of official fortifications.

What future now for the Cité on the Hill?

⌘ CHAPTER 54 ⌘

The Rosetta Stone

*N*apoleon Bonaparte was born to a noble Italian family in Ajaccio, but moved to France to train for the army. One examiner noted his deep interest in the 'abstract sciences, little curious as to the others; a thorough knowledge of mathematics and geography'.

In 1795, Bonaparte successfully defended the Revolutionary government in Paris from royalist sympathisers and the following year led the successful Italian campaign that brought an end to over 1,000 years of Venetian independence. In March 1798, he launched a new campaign to invade and take possession of Egypt, a province of the Ottoman Empire. He tried to gain popular support, issuing proclamations that portrayed him as a liberator from Ottoman oppression and praising Islam.

As well as an impressive military force, Napoleon assembled a huge corps of scientists to accompany his Egyptian campaign. Some have suggested that he went to North Africa deliberately in search of ancient knowledge or that the lavish team of academics was a cover – a kind of Enlightenment smokescreen – designed to hide his imperialist motives. In any case, in 1798 Napoleon founded the Institut de l'Egypte and about fifty members of his expedition became founder members. Then, on 15 July 1799, came the discovery.

Napoleon's troops were improving the fortifications at Fort Julien near the city of Rosetta, an Egyptian port known today as Rashid. A French captain named Bouchard discovered a dark pinkish-grey slab of granite carved with text in three different scripts. It was about the size of a gravestone but thicker, nearly 28 centimetres. An intelligent man, Bouchard immediately realised its potential importance and showed it to his general, who sent it on to the institute. It arrived in August 1799.

Study of the Rosetta Stone revealed two languages – Egyptian and

Greek. Plus, the Egyptian was written in two different scripts, demotic and hieratic, making three sets of carved writing in all. The Rosetta Stone was dated to 196 BCE and casts were taken. Then, in 1801, the French had to surrender to British forces. They tried to hide the Rosetta Stone but the British found it and, in 1802, they brought it back to the British Museum in London.

In London, the Rosetta Stone attracted the attention of the brilliant British polymath Thomas Young. Because of his extraordinary breadth and depth of knowledge, seemingly on all subjects known to humankind, Thomas was known as Phenomenon Young. He completed a translation of the demotic text on the Rosetta Stone in 1814 and made good progress towards deciphering the hieratic text. His work was published in 1818 in an article for the *Encyclopaedia Britannica*. More work led him to deduce certain common words in the texts, such as 'Egyptian' and 'temple'. But the conclusive work was accomplished by a Frenchman who was obliged to work not from the Stone itself but from the casts made before the French surrender in Egypt: Jean-François Champollion.

Champollion was born in 1790 in Figeac in southwest France. He found school difficult and seems to have been unable at first to distinguish between the separate letters of French or Latin words, seeing them instead as little pictures. Of course, this odd 'learning difficulty' meant he was ideally suited to the study of hieroglyphs and, greatly helped by his elder brother, Jacques-Joseph, he mastered perhaps a dozen languages while only a child.

Champollion realised that in order to decipher hieroglyphics, he would first have to learn Coptic, a language descended from ancient Egyptian but written with a modified Greek alphabet. In 1805, just fifteen years old, only six years after the discovery of the Rosetta Stone, he gained the assistance of a former Coptic monk who gave him lessons and brought him books. He soon presented a paper on Coptic to the Grenoble Academy.

In around 1807, Champollion concluded that – contrary to church doctrine – Moses could not have written the first five books of the Old Testament as they were not written in Egyptian. Champollion identified seven demotic signs in the Coptic text of the Rosetta Stone, then managed to work out which hieroglyphic signs they were derived from. This meant he could begin to make guesses about the structure of sentences and paragraphs in the hieroglyphic text and develop theories about the meanings of other symbols.

Hieroglyphs can be written from right to left or left to right – or even top to bottom. The most common format is from right to left. Because many hieroglyphs are asymmetrical – animals or people, for example – once you know what you are looking for, it is quite easy to see the direction in which they should be read. Another complication comes from the complete absence of spaces between words or punctuation and the fact that some characters have no 'meaning' but simply serve to indicate the end of a word made up of several preceding hieroglyphs.

Champollion decided:

C'est un système complexe, une écriture tout à la fois figurative, symbolique et phonétique, dans un même texte, une même phrase, je dirais presque dans un même mot.

It is a complex system. The writing is, simultaneously, figurative, symbolic and phonetic, in the same text, the same phrase. I might almost say in the same word.

On making his breakthrough, Champollion was so excited he ran to the house of his brother, Jacques-Joseph, burst in and gasped: *'Je tiens l'affaire!'* ('I've got it!') Then he collapsed unconscious on the floor. The date was 14 September 1822. He was the first person in more than a millennium to have a fluent understanding of Egyptian writing.

Of course, there were disputes as to who should get the credit for deciphering hieroglyphic writing, with the French and the British each supporting 'their' man. Young praised Champollion's work but claimed part of the credit as the Frenchman had based his analysis on his articles. Later the feud ended when Champollion, now a curator at the Louvre, allowed Young access to demotic texts stored there.

In 1828, Champollion led a joint Franco-Tuscan expedition to Egypt, voyaging upstream on the Nile and studying a huge range of relics. In the Valley of the Kings, his men removed two mirror-image wall paintings from the tomb of Seti I, a barbarous act of treasure-hunting. The pieces are today exhibited in the Louvre and the museum of Florence. Soon after, in 1832, Jean-François Champollion died of apoplexy at forty-one years old, his last works being completed for publication by his brother. He was buried in the Père Lachaise cemetery in Paris.

In 1858, three undergraduates of the University of Pennsylvania, whose

Philomathean Society holds a life-size cast of the Rosetta Stone, published the first complete English translations. On the left-hand side of the original can still be seen the contemporary inscription 'Captured in Egypt by the British Army in 1801'. On the right-hand side it says: 'Presented by King George III.' It has remained in the British Museum continuously, apart from a two-year period towards the end of World War I when it was moved, for fear of bomb damage, to a Postal Tube Railway station 50 feet underground.

In July 2003, Dr Zahi Hawass of the Supreme Council of Antiquities in Cairo, told the media: 'If the British want to be remembered, if they want to restore their reputation, they should volunteer to return the Stone because it is the icon of our Egyptian identity.'

The panels looted by Champollion from the tomb of Seti I are still displayed in Florence and Paris; the Rosetta Stone is still in the British Museum.

⌸ CHAPTER 55 ⌸
Carcassonne Reborn

*O*nce the Emperor Napoleon had Carcassonne removed from the official roster of fortifications, the Cité fell further into a state of pitiful disrepair. By 1830 the great twin towers of the Porte Narbonnaise were roofless and undermined. The old stones were cannibalised by local people, many of them used to extend the parasitic shanty towns within the *lices*. By 1840 the bishop's palace and the cloister of the basilica of Saint-Nazaire had disappeared and the local authorities decided to officially list the building to prevent further vandalism and theft of its materials. Below the walls, too, houses had been built or extended using stones 'salvaged' from the Cité. In 1844, an exhaustive schedule of essential repairs was drawn up, including newly sculpted identical gargoyles to replace the worn or broken originals.

The Cité's economy was prosperous, founded on textiles. The flat land between the two rings of mighty fortifications was used as a drying ground for the textile industry that employed many of the 1,400 people living in the fortress. Even the moat of the Château Comtal was used to lay out great sheets of cloth in the bright sun. The shanties in the *lices* and the popular neighbourhoods beneath the walls – Trivalle and Barbacane – housed many weavers and self-employed seamstresses who transformed the great sheets into shirts and smocks and pillowcases and other linens.

The project to renovate the basilica lasted until 1867 and was an enormous undertaking – both financial and in the mobilisation of a large and skilled workforce. But it was only a fragment of the Cité. Still the walls and towers were left unprotected from the elements. In the midst of the renovation, a new project was launched.

The condition of the fortress declined so far that in 1849 the French government floated the idea that it should be demolished. Uproar ensued. A popular campaign was set up by the mayor of Carcassonne, Jean-Pierre Cros-Mayrevieille, a man with a deep love for the past. He was supported by the very first French *inspecteur* of historic monuments, Prosper Mérimée. The campaign was successful and an architect by the name of Eugène Emmanuel Viollet-le-Duc – the man responsible for the ongoing restoration of the basilica of Saint-Nazaire – was commissioned not just to halt the depredations but to renovate the entire citadel.

Viollet-le-Duc was born in 1814 in Paris. His father was a book-loving civil servant and his mother ran a salon that attracted literary celebrities such as Stendhal and Sainte-Beuve. The young Eugène's education was taken in hand by his mother's brother – also Eugène, a painter and amateur academic. Young Eugène had a rebellious nature. He refused to attend the conservative Ecole des Beaux-Arts and took part in street barricades in the July Revolution of 1830. Yet five years later, on his return from a study trip to Italy, Prosper Mérimée gave Viollet-le-Duc the job of restoring the Romanesque Vézelay abbey. He went on to conduct a series of refurbishments on the cathedral of Notre-Dame in Paris, including

the monumental south rose window. Napoleon III com- missioned him to design a railway carriage in a 14th- century Gothic style.

Viollet-le-Duc was as important to the French Gothic revival in architecture as Pugin, the designer of the pointed Gothic palace of Westminster, was in England. He had an enormous influence on the Catalan architect Antoni Gaudí. Through drawings and sketches he created an invaluable record of buildings too far gone to be restored and earmarked for demolition. He also studied medieval furniture, dress, musical instruments and so on.

Viollet-le-Duc

He had a second career in the military and took part in the defence of Paris in the Franco-Prussian War of 1870–1. Some of his military writings inspired the disastrous confidence placed by the French military in the World War I fortifications known as the Maginot Line.

Although he worked on many Gothic medieval buildings with sensitivity and respect, Viollet-le-Duc was a pragmatic man whose choice of materials or designs did not necessarily reflect strict historical authenticity. In Carcassonne, he started in 1853 with the west and southwest walls, then moved quickly on to the twin towers of the Porte Narbonnaise. Swiftly, his work provoked strong criticism. He needed to get the structures roofed to save them from further damage from the elements. But the rooftops of the Midi generally have a very shallow pitch, because the low rainfall and rare snow mean they don't have to be very steep to throw the weather off. The typical – in fact, ubiquitous – local roofing material is clay tile. Viollet-le-Duc chose to have his repairs carried out in slate, erected on steep conical roofs – like the hats of medieval ladies – just as he had in northern France.

Viollet-le-Duc wanted the shanty dwellings removed from the *lices* of the Cité. There were 122 houses in the gap between the walls and it took some years for the clearance to be completed. Each house was compulsorily purchased by the state – some for 2,000 francs each – and demolished. Many had vegetable and herbs gardens which also had to be removed. In 1864, the Laffon family deserted the mud-and-stone house they had built with their own hands in the shadow of the Tour de la Vade, which, incredibly, was still used as an army powder depot. But the inhabitants of the *lices* were still numerous enough to successfully petition for the mayor of Carcassonne to install eight gas lamps in 1866.

When Viollet-le-Duc died in 1879, the restoration of the Cité was still incomplete. On his death, he left sheaves of notes and instructions for his son to follow at Carcassonne but, a little like painting the Golden Gate Bridge, the work, even today, can never be said to be truly finished.

⌘ EPILOGUE ⌘

In the seventeen years since we bought our house in Carcassonne, the region has changed enormously. Commercial flights into the tiny airport have brought many more holidaymakers, most of them English, but also German, Belgian and Dutch. Dusty old car parks have been refurbished and decked with café tables. The banks of the river have been landscaped and planted with rich, bright flowers. Tumbledown homes have been bought and done up, geraniums in their window boxes, oleander by the door. The Occitan names for the old towns have appeared on the road signs. Carcasonna for Carcassonne, Fanjaus for Fanjeaux.

The medieval walled Cité is – if it is possible – even more popular than ever before, jam-packed throughout the holiday season with families and coach parties, inspecting the *château*, the tiny streets and alleyways, medieval bricks from those parts of the walls restored in the mid-19th century. Every now and again, someone goes by holding a copy of *Labyrinth*, and I feel both grateful for the inspiration that Carcassonne brought me and a little guilty.

In the ruins of the defeated strongholds of Languedoc, visitor centres have been built selling a fantastic range of gorgeous and informative guides to the catastrophe of the Crusade against the Cathars. In the last two decades, is it too romantic, too fanciful to say that, at last, history has been reclaimed by those who, 800 years ago, were defeated? Here and there, it is possible to meet people who, inspired by the continuing historical research, style themselves Cathars.

I set out to write a story that wove together the lives of two women, divided by eight centuries. But that story was itself woven into the pattern of real events as they happened, battle by battle, date by date. And luckily for me, in Chartres, in Jerusalem, on the banks of the Nile, at Montségur and in Carcassonne, history is always present.

Kate Mosse
Carcassonne, January 2007

⌘ APPENDICES ⌘
Pictures Credits

▦ APPENDICES ▦
Acknowledgements

Among the many historians who have researched and retold the history of Catharism, I would like to acknowledge, above all, the work of Jean Duvernoy and Anne Brenon. Genevieve Pegg at Orion is an excellent editor; Mark Lucas a splendid agent. This book exists, however, because in *Labyrinth*, Kate made history live.